101 MYSTICS OF INDIA

BOOKS BY V.K. SUBRAMANIAN

Astrology/Palmistry

Predictive Planets and Presaging Palms

Biography

The Great Ones (Volumes 1 to 4)
101 Mystics of India

Economy/Finance

The Indian Financial System
Introspection for India—A Paradigm for Progress

Fiction

A Feeling for Feminism

Health Management

The Holistic Way to Health, Happiness and Harmony
Heavenly Living Here and Now

Indian Culture

Art Shrines of Ancient India
Sacred Songs of India (Volumes 1 to 10)
Wondrous Whispers of Wisdom from Ancient India (Volumes 1 to 3)
Maxims of Chanakya
Mystic Songs of Meera

Religion & Philosophy

Sri Rudraprasna
Saundaryalahari of Sankaracharya
Sivanandalahari of Sankaracharya
The Upanishads and the Bible
Raja Yoga—The Royal Road to Revelation

101 MYSTICS OF INDIA

V.K. SUBRAMANIAN

ABHINAV PUBLICATIONS
abhinav publications
NEW DELHI

Cataloging in Publication Data—DK
Courtesy: D.K. Agencies (P) Ltd.
<docinfo@dkagencies.com>

Subramanian, V. K. (Vadakaymadam Krishnier), 1930-
101 mystics of India / V.K. Subramanian.
p. cm.
Includes index.
ISBN 8170174457

1. Mystics—India—Biography. I. Title.
II. Title: One hundred one mystics of India.

DDC 291.422 092 21

First published in India 2006

Publishers
Shakti Malik
Abhinav Publications
E-37, Hauz Khas
New Delhi-110016 (INDIA)
Phones: 26566387, 26562784, 26524658
Fax: 91-11-26857009
e-mail: shakti@nde.vsnl.net.in
website: http//www.abhinavexports.com

ISBN 81-7017-445-7

Lasertypeset by
Onkar Digital Studio
Rohini, Delhi-110085

Printed at
D.K. Fine Art Press Pvt. Ltd.
Ashok Vihar, Delhi

To
Renu and Nagraj
who lead truly spiritual lives,
while living in a luxurious,
materialistic ambience

Cover Illustration: Bronze sculpture of Sundarar, Saivite mystic saint, discovered in 1908 at Siva Temple 5, Polonnaruva.

Courtesy: The National Museum, Colombo.

Cover Design and Illustrations in the book by V.K. Subramanian

CONTENTS

INTRODUCTION

I have pleasure and pride in presenting *101 Mystics of India* to my readers.

Who is a Mystic?

The *American Heritage Dictionary of the English Language* defines a mystic as one who *experiences an immediate consciousness of the transcendent or ultimate reality or God and describes the experience of such communion.*

The expression of experience of a mystic can be the establishment of a philosophy or religion, the creation of a monumental work of art like an epic, the composition of devotional lyrics set to melodious music by themselves and others, or observance of an inspiring silence which can spark spiritual awakening in devotees.

The mystics of India cover all the categories.

Thus, we have *Gautama Buddha* and *Mahavira* establishing new religions as a result of their mystical experience; sages like *Valmiki* and *Veda Vyasa* writing epics; *Kalidasa* creating immortal plays and poems; *Patanjali, Sankara, Ramanuja* and *Madhvacharya* propounding diverse philosophical doctrines; and the innumerable mystics of the *Bhakti* movement pouring out their mystical experience in soulful musical compositions.

Under the last category come the *Alwars* (like *Nammalwar, Perialwar, Tirumangai Azhwar, Kulasekhara Perumal* and others) and *Nayanmars* (like *Sundarar, Appar, Manikkavachakar, Tirujnanasambandhar* and others); the saints of *Maharashtra* like *Tukaram, Eknath, Jnaneswar* and *Samartha Ramadas* and the stalwarts like *Tulsidas, Surdas, Kabir, Vidyapati, Chandidas, Sant Raidas, Jayadeva, Chaitanya, Vallabhacharya, Narsi Mehta, Rahim, Raskhan, Dadu Dayal* and *Bulleh Shah*; the musical composers of the South like *Tyagaraja, Muttuswami Dikshitar, Syama Sastri, Papanasam Sivan, Pattanam Subramania Iyer, Mysore Vasudevachar, Swati Tirunal, Harikesanallur Muthiah Bhagavatar* and scores of other Carnatic music composers like *Oottukkadu Venkatasubba Iyer, Gopalakrishna Bharati, Neelakantha Sivan,* etc.

The sprouting of mystics in India has defied the constrictions of region, language, gender and time.

Prominent mystics from *Karnataka* include Veerasaivite leaders like *Devara Dasimayya, Allama Prabhu* and *Basavanna* and such outstanding devotees like *Kanakadasa* and *Purandharadasa*.

Mystics from *Andhra Pradesh* include: *Annamacharya, Kshetrajna, Bhadrachala Ramadas, Sadasiva Brahmendra* and *Narayana Teertha*.

Mystics from *Punjab* are the Sikh Gurus like *Guru Nanak, Guru Arjan Dev, Guru Amar Das, Guru Ramdas* and *Guru Tegh Bahadur*.

Among the mystics from *Kerala* most prominent are *Poontanam, Narayana Bhattadiri, Ezhuttacchan, Narayana Guru, Bilwa Mangal* and *Iriyamman Tampi*.

Among the great *Tamil* mystics come *Agastya, Avvaiyar, Tirumoolar, Arunagirinathar, Kamban,* the creator of the classic *Kamba Ramayana, Ilango Adikal,* the author of *Silappadikaram,* Tiruvalluvar, author of the famous *Tirukkural, Pattinattar, Tayumanavar, Muttu Tandavar, Abhirami Bhattar, Appayya Dikshitar* and *Vedanta Desikan*.

Illustrating the irrelevance of region, come *Sankaradeva* from *Assam, Bhima Bhoi,* the tribal chief of *Orissa, Shahji*

Maharaja of Tanjore and *Ramprasad Sen* of *Bengal.*

Among the women mystics come *Karaikkal Ammaiyar, Andal, Mahadevi Akka, Jana Bai, Meera* and *Lal Ded* (*Lalla Yogeswari*) of *Kashmir.*

Continuing the unbroken chain down the centuries, we have in modern times such stalwarts like *Sri Aurobindo, Ramakrishna Paramahamsa, Swami Vivekananda, Subramania Bharati, Suddhananda Bharati, Rabindranath Tagore, Ramalinga Swamigal, Ramana Maharishi, Paramacharya of Kanchi* and *Jiddu Krishnamurthy.*

In compiling this list of 101 mystics of India, I am definitely guilty of omission of important savants. I may be forgiven for my incomplete, whimsical and arbitrary selection.

I may also be forgiven for the *shortness* of presentation. I can, in my defence, only refer to the allegory mentioned by *Anton Chekhov* to *George Sand*:

"Why are your songs so short?" the bird was asked.

"Are you short of breath?"

The bird replied: "No. I have many songs to sing and I want the world to hear them all."

Chennai, India **V.K. Subramanian**

AGASTYA

AGASTYA (2500 B.C.)

There are so many myths and legends about Agastya in the *purānas* and the epics, that one would have doubted his physical existence but for his works which are very much with us.

Sage Agastya, who was dwarfish in appearance, is considered the doyen of Tamil mystics and the father of the Tamil language. He is to the Tamil language what Panini was to Sanskrit.

The Tamil grammar *Tolkāpyam*, one of the oldest grammars in the world, was written by one of the twelve disciples of Agastya. The songs on Ganesa composed by Agastya in Tamil are found in his work "*Kāryasiddhi Malai*".

Agastya is famous for teaching the "*Āditya Hṛdaya*" mantra to Sri Rama on the eve of his battle with the demon Ravana. Rama is believed to have won victory because of the power of the prayer to the Sun taught by Agastya.

Even today millions recite this prayer to achieve success and get rid of eye problems.

Agastya's songs on Ganesa are also believed to ensure success in all undertakings.

Kāryasiddhimalai literally means "garland (of songs) which ensures success in undertakings".

Other works attributed to Agastya are:

1. *Agastya Gita* (in the Varahapurana)
2. *Agastya Samhita* (in Skandapurana)
3. *Siva Samhita* (in Bhaskara Samhita)
4. *Dvaida Nirnaya Tantra.*

VALMIKI

VALMIKI (14th-15th Century B.C.)

Valmiki, the author of the epic *Ramayana,* bears comparison with *Homer.* According to *Sri Aurobindo, Valmiki, Vyasa* and *Kalidasa* are the Indian equivalents of *Homer, Dante* and *Shakespeare.*

The story of *Rama,* the ideal son and Ruler, *Sita,* the ideal wife, *Bharata* and *Lakshmana,* the ideal brothers and *Hanuman,* the ideal devotee, has been so beautifully stated in the epic poem of *Ramayana* that even in the remotest village in India, even the most illiterate man, woman or child is familiar with the characters and situations in the story. The credit for this goes to the poetic and dramatic genius of Valmiki. Though subsequent poets like *Tulsidas* and *Kamban* have restated the story in their own style, their inspiration has been Valmiki.

No poem in the world is superior to the *Ramayana* of Valmiki, says *Aurobindo.* How *Ratnakar* the bandit became the poet Valmiki is well known. Once when he tried to rob a sage, of his meagre belongings, he was told that no one else but he would suffer the consequences of his misdeeds. Repentant and reformed he asked the sage for the way out of sin. He was told to recite *Mara, Mara* (reverse of *Rama*).

The bandit sat in penance and recited the mantra and forgot the world. An anthill enveloped him. When he was dug out, he was a realised soul and called *Vālmiki* (one who came out of Valmike (Sanskrit for anthill).

The urge to write *Ramayana* was triggered by Valmiki's sensitive reaction to the wailing of a bird, whose mate was killed by a hunter.

The ideal society portrayed so realistically in the *Ramayana* by Valmiki made *Gandhiji* name the Utopia he envisaged for India: *Rāma Rājya*!

VEDA VYASA

VEDA VYASA (13th Century B.C.)

Veda Vyasa, the author of the epics, *Mahābhārata* and *Bhāgavata* and several Puranas, was the son of Sage *Parāsara* and the fisherwoman *Satyavati.*

The late sage of Kanchi, Paramacharya, said of Vyasa:

"There is no means of approach to the Supreme which does not find a place in one or other works of Vyasa. Bhagavan Vyasa is a *Mārgadarśi* (Pathfinder) without an equal in any country or age."

Veda Vyasa was a great Yogi, great *Jnāni,* great mystical devotee and lover of God, apart from being a great poet and philosopher.

The greatness of Veda Vyasa lies in the fact that the words of prayer, philosophy and wisdom he puts into the mouth of characters he has created in his epic works, have come to be identified as the expressions of the characters themselves. Thus the famous *Bhagavat Gita,* which is like the Bible of India, is universally accepted as the words of wisdom spoken by Lord Krishna, though the author is Veda Vyasa.

Some of the songs composed by Vyasa like the *Gopikāgitam,* song of the Gopis yearning for Lord Krishna, *Durgāstotram,* a prayer of Yudhishtira in the Mahabharata, *Prayer to Lord Krishna* by Bhishma and other prayers in the *Bhāgavatam* and other puranas are more identified with the mystical devotion of the characters, though there is no mistaking whose deep devotion and mysticism these songs express.

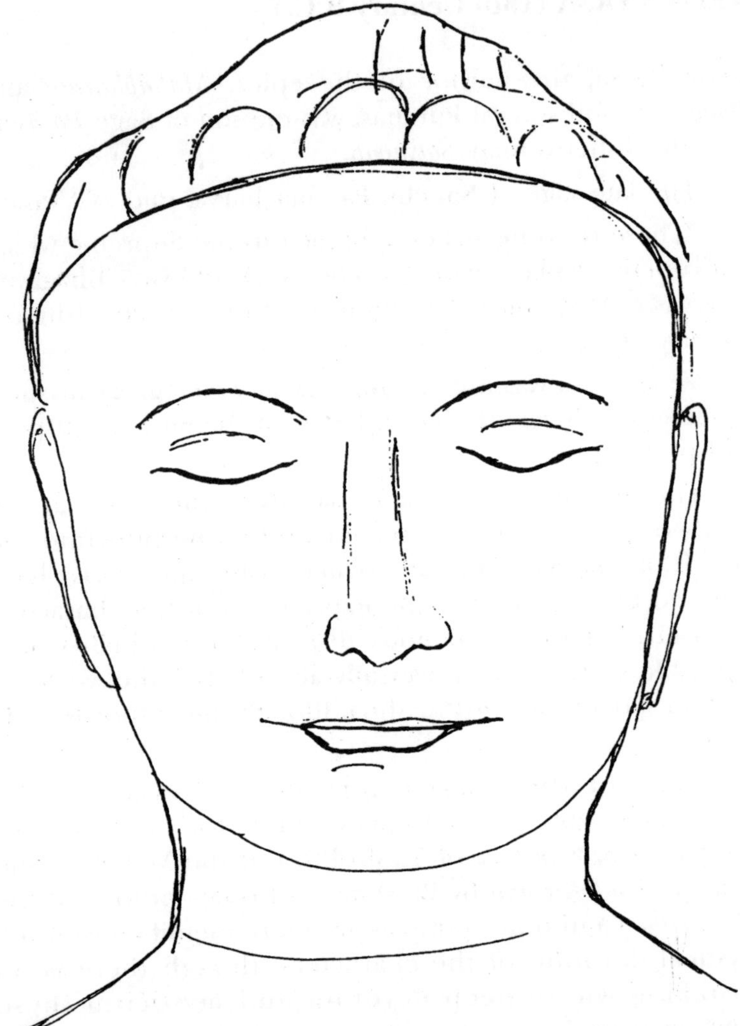

MAHAVIRA

MAHAVIRA (599-526 B.C.)

Mahavira is the moulder of the Jain religion as it exists today. He was the last and 24th pathfinder (*Tirthankara*). His contribution to Jainism was so outstanding that he is often considered the founder of Jainism, as Buddha of Buddhism.

The lives of these two great sons of India were very similar. Both were born in affluent families, got married, had a child and then in the prime of life renounced the world and went in search of spiritual knowledge.

Mahavira attained enlightenment at the age of fortytwo and preached the tenets of Jainism for the next 30 years till his death.

The teachings of Mahavira can be summarised in three words: *Ahimsa* (non-violence), *Karmavāda* (theory of Karma), and *Syadvāda* (the art of looking at the other person from his or her point of view).

The doctrine of non-violence of Mahavira encompassed both human and non-human beings and spread the cult of vegetarianism in society. This was adopted by the majority of Hindus as well. The theory of Karma, put in a nutshell: "As you sow, so you reap" has also become part of Hindu religion and philosophy.

Syadvāda or looking at other people from their point of view created a tolerant attitude to other religious beliefs. This also has become an integral part of Hinduism.

Mahavira preached five vows for spiritual liberation: *non-injury, truthfulness, abstention from stealing, non-attachment* and *celibacy.*

He asserted that "everyone is capable of attaining perfection". Karmic bondage can be destroyed by self-purification.

Ends and means are interconnected (a view which guided Gandhiji all his life).

"Focussing on the spirit implies an indifference to the body." Mahavira stood for the abolition of all distinctions based on caste, colour and sex. The Jainism he moulded was a spiritual democracy.

Over 3.5 million Jains faithfully and zealously practise even today the preachings of Mahavira.

GAUTAMA BUDDHA

GAUTAMA BUDDHA (566-486 B.C.)

Gautama Buddha, the founder of Buddhism, was the royal Prince Siddharta, who at the age of thirty, renounced his luxurious life and turned an ascetic, seeking a solution to the problem of sorrow which afflicted life on earth.

He came to the conclusion that neither self-indulgence nor self-mortification was the answer.

He stressed the four noble truths: sorrow, the cause of sorrow, the ending of sorrow and the paths leading thereto.

He preached the eightfold middle path for liberation from sorrow: *right views, right aspirations, right speech, right conduct, right living, right effort, right recollection* and *right meditation.*

Gautama Buddha advocated universal love, compassion, sympathetic joy and equanimity.

The great one who said: "*Ahimsa paramo dharmah*" (non-violence is the supreme duty) used to tell his disciples:

"When a man has pity on all living creatures, then only is he noble."

"Never in this world can hatred be stilled by hatred, it will be stilled only by non-hatred—that is the Law Eternal", was his constant exhortation.

Once a woman, who lost her only son, approached Buddha for solace. He asked her to bring a little mustard seed from any house, where no person has yet died.

The woman found that there was no family where death had not entered and realised that it was the law of all things that they will pass away.

Grief arises out of attachment. Hence the only way to happiness is detachment to earthly possessions.

PATANJALI

PATANJALI (200-150 B.C.)

Maharishi Patanjali's great contribution to human civilization is his *magnum opus* "*The Yoga Sutras*" comprising 196 sutras or maxims, dealing with the "*Science of the mind*".

Patanjali's *Yoga Sutras* are the foundation of *Raja Yoga*, or the path of meditation for God realization.

The unique attraction of *Raja Yoga* is that it is a spiritual path available to everyone, irrespective of religion, since the mind is universal.

Patanjali's *Yoga Sutras* is the *scriptural text of Raja Yoga* and has four chapters:

Chapter One (51 Maxims) dealing with *Samādhi* (Superconscious state).

Chapter Two (55 Maxims) dealing with *Sādhana* or practice.

Chapter Three (56 Maxims) dealing with *Vibhūti* or occult powers.

Chapter Four (34 Maxims) dealing with *Kaivalya* or liberation.

The key message of Patanjali is: *Yoga is cessation of mental activity and when the mind becomes a vacuum, the seer in us gets established in his true form.*

All the techniques of meditation and approaches to self-realization are based on Patanjali's methodology for stilling the mind.

According to Patanjali, the external world is but the gross form of the internal or subtle. The finer is always the cause, the grosser the effect. So the external world is the effect, the internal the cause...The man who has discovered and learnt how to manipulate internal forces will get the whole of Nature under his control.

The system of Yoga, taught by Patanjali, is the key to the realm of divinity inside man and can be termed the *high technology of the science of spirituality*.

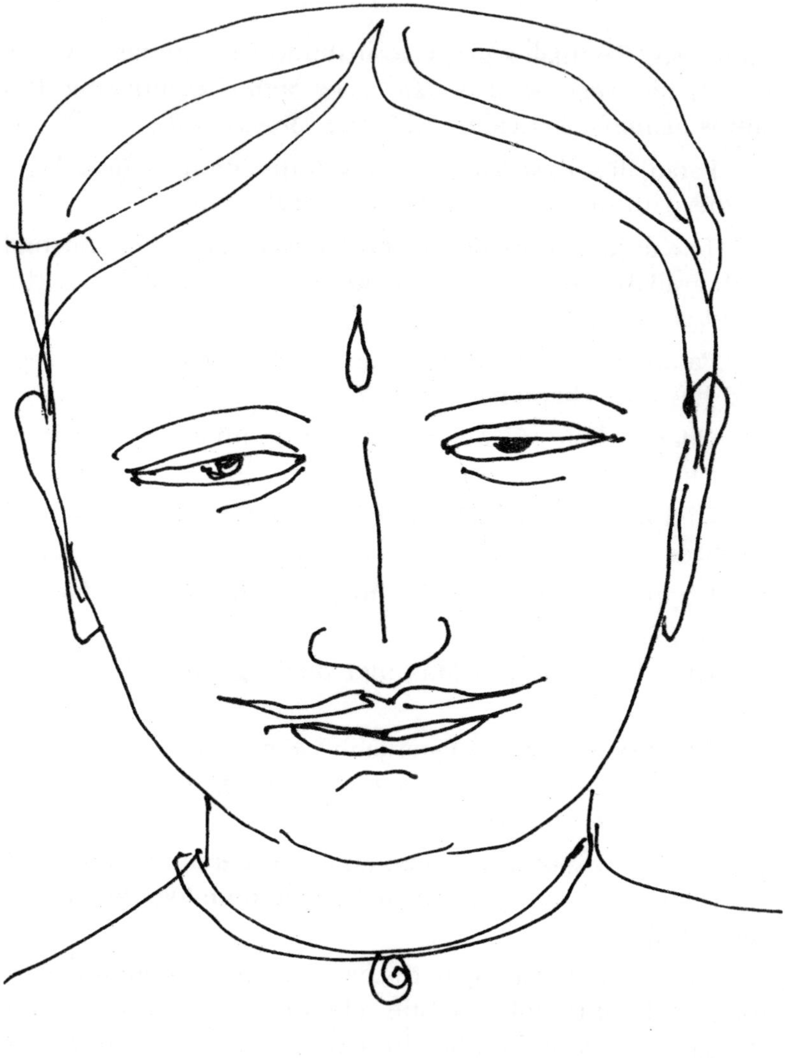

ILANGO ADIKAL

ILANGO ADIKAL (2nd Century A.D.)

Ilango Adikal, the author of the classic Tamil work, *Silappadikaram*, is, according to Subramania Bharati, one of the Trinity of great Tamil poets, the other two being *Tiruvalluvar*, author of the famous *Tirukkural* and *Kamban*, the author of the *Tamil Ramayana.*

Ilango Adikal was a contemporary of *Sattanar*, the author of *Manimekalai*, another Tamil classic.

Ilango was born as the second son of King Ceralatan of the Cera dynasty, his elder brother being the famous Ceran Senguttavan.

At a young age, Ilango renounced royalty and became an ascetic. Hence he came to be known as Ilango Adikal.

Ilango belonged to the Sangam period in Tamil literature. Exact date of his life is controversial. Western scholars believe he lived in the 7th or 8th century A.D., while Eastern scholars think he lived in the 2nd century A.D.

Ilango Adikal spent all his life in a monastery, called *Kunavayilkottam*, outside the Cera capital, *Vanji*, devoting his life to philosophy and literature.

The songs of Ilango Adikal deal with Ilango's adulation of Krishna, who is also Rama and Vishnu. They reveal his elegant simple style and powerful imagery, born out of his devotion to God.

TIRUMOOLAR

TIRUMOOLAR (3rd-5th Century A.D.)

Tirumoolar is deemed the doyen of mystics and seers of Tamil Nadu.

The spiritual path shown by Tirumoolar became, nurtured by the *Nayanmars,* the system of devotion famous as *Saiva Siddhanta,* which was propagated by a number of mystics, the latest being Ramalinga Swamigal who lived in the 19th century A.D.

Tirumoolar's *magnum opus* is *Tirumantiram,* a work comprising 3000 verses.

Tirumoolar's most profound dictum was: *Anbe Sivam,* "God is Love". Adoration of God is hence cardinal to Tirumoolar.

The other famous dictum of Tirumoolar is: *Yan Petra Inbam Peruka Ivvaiyakam* viz. "May this world experience the bliss I have experienced."

The third dictum of Tirumoolar is: *Onre Kulamum Oruvane Daivamum*: "Mankind is one family. There is only one God."

Tirumoolar also propagated the view that the body, being the temple of God, was to be treasured as a divine gift.

Tirumoolar realised the presence of God within and adored Him as the immanent presence.

Tirumoolar's emphasis on God being Love, the oneness of humankind and the dignity of the body to be used for spiritual uplift and the immanence of God within, is a unique contribution in the spiritual history of India and justifies the encomium conferred on him by *Tāyumanavar* that he was the "*Emperor of Meditators*".

TIRUVALLUVAR

TIRUVALLUVAR (5th Century A.D.)

Tiruvalluvar, the Tamil saint who authored the immortal *Tirukkural,* has been called the *Bard of the universal man,* the *Solomon of Tamil Literature,* etc.

The *Tirukkural,* containing 1330 maxims, in 133 chapters of 10 couplets each, preaches moral values of a high ethical order.

Albert Schweitzer, the great philosopher, said of Tiruvalluvar's *magnum opus*: "With sure strokes, the *Kural* draws the ideal of simple ethical humanity. On the most varied questions concerning the conduct of man to himself and to the world its utterances are characterised by nobility and good sense. *There hardly exists in the literature of the world a collection of maxims in which we find such lofty wisdom.*" Mahatma Gandhi considered the *Tirukkural* as *one of the highest and purest expressions of human thought.*

Tiruvalluvar lived in the 2nd century B.C. according to Oriental scholars and 5th century A.D. according to Western scholars.

He was a weaver by profession and lived a contented householder's life with his devoted wife *Vasuki.*

The first verse of *Tirukkural* refers to God as the *Primordial One* thus: "*The letter A is the first among all letters. So too is God, the First among all lives.*"

Other samples of his wit and wisdom:

They will say: "*The flute is sweet, the lute is sweet, who have not heard the lispings of their kids.*"

"*Death is like sleep; birth is like waking up.*"

"*The capacity to hear is the asset of assets; it outshines all other assets.*"

KARAIKKAL AMMAIYAR

KARAIKKAL AMMAIYAR (5th Century A.D.)

Myth and legend obscure the biographical details about Karaikkal Ammaiyar.

The only source available for her life-sketch is the *Periya Puranam* of Cekkilar.

The undisputed fact is that she was a Saivite saint, madly in love with her chosen Deity, Siva.

Her maiden name was *Punitavatiyar.* She was born in Karaikkal, the daughter of a businessman.

Even as a child, she developed deep love for God.

Though she was married, according to Vedic rites, her husband, afraid of her spiritual powers, left her and went away.

The story goes that Karaikkal Ammaiyar sought and obtained a spirit form, by the grace of God.

Her devotional songs are melodious and simple, reflecting her adoration of the Lord.

Karaikkal Ammaiyar is considered one of the most prominent Saivite poet-saints of South India.

KALIDASA

KALIDASA (6th Century A.D.)

Kalidasa is the national poet of India and the greatest Sanskrit poet.

He is to Sanskrit literature what William Shakespeare is to English literature.

Kalidasa has composed the lyrics *Ritusamhāra* and *Meghadūta,* the two epics *Raghuvamsa* and *Kumārasambhava,* and the three plays *Malavikagnimitra, Vikramorvaśiya* and *Śākuntalam.*

How does this romantic poet find a place among the mystic saints of India, is a question which can legitimately be raised.

The answer is contained in Kalidasa's own dictum: "*Nanṛshi kurute kāvyam*"—"One who is not a sage cannot create a poem."

Though Kalidasa dealt with the sensory emotions of princes and princesses and celestial beings, there is no denying the fact that he was an ardent devotee of God, whom he worshipped as the Primordial Father-Mother.

The benedictory verses at the beginning of his works bring out his ardent devotion to God.

The legend about his transformation from a dumb shepherd to a proliferous poet by the grace of the Divine Mother is too well known to merit repetition. The composition *Symālādandakam* is his homage in gratitude.

The sensual imagery used by Kalidasa in spiritual devotion is not uncommon among the mystics of India. Jayadeva, Vidyapati and even Sankaracharya have used this in their devotional songs.

PERIALWAR

PERIALWAR (6th-7th Century A.D.)

Perialwar was born in Srivilliputtoor, Tamil Nadu, India, in a Brahmin family. His original name was *Vishnuchitta.* He was the foster parent of the famous Andal, whose birth date has been ascribed to the middle 7th century by scholars. We can hence safely assume Perialwar to have been born some time in late 6th century or early 7th century A.D.

He used to make garlands of flowers and take them to the local temple in Srivilliputtoor, where he prayed daily with intense devotion.

Perialwar was fascinated by the childhood exploits of Sri Krishna and developed devotion and love for God, incarnated as Krishna. And he sang of Krishna, the child Deity, with maternal love. He was more concerned about the welfare of child Krishna than his own! Because his love and devotion excelled that of other Alwars, he was named *Perialwar* or the Great Alwar.

He installed the image of his chosen Deity in his heart and offered songs of love to Him.

Apart from his native *Srivilliputtoor,* Perialwar visited temples at *Tirukkottiyoor, Tiruvarangam, Tiruvellarai, Tirumaliruncholai* and sang his songs of devotion and love.

Tirupallandu is Perialwar's most famous composition.

Perialwar was the doyen of the Vaishnavite bards, known as *Alwars,* whose devotional songs are called *Paasurams.*

"*Can anything equal the art of Pallandu? Can anyone equal Perialwar?*" goes the popular Vaishnavite adage.

KULASEKHARA PERUMAL

KULASEKHARA PERUMAL (6th-7th Century A.D.)

Kulasekhara Perumal is one of the twelve *Alwars,* the Vaishnavite religious poets of Tamil Nadu.

The *Alwars* are so called because they are deemed to be "*immersed*" in the love of God.

The Alwars came from different backgrounds and social strata. There were Brahmins, Kshatriyas, non-Brahmins, cultivators and Harijans among them, but the intoxicating love of God unified them.

Kulasekhara was a King in Kerala. Though he was a competent ruler, he became preoccupied with spirituality and sacred lore.

The intensity of Kulasekhara's devotion is reflected in his songs.

In some of his songs, he has expressed a desire to be a stone in the Tirupati temple of Lord Venkateswara.

His involvement in the myths and legends of Lord Krishna and Lord Rama has produced some exquisite devotional poetry.

In one song, he identifies himself with *Devaki,* the biological mother of Krishna, from whom Krishna was taken away to Gokula where Nanda and Yasoda, the foster parents, looked after him.

Kulasekhara expresses Devaki's desolation at being separated from her child and yearning for union with him again.

This is the same sense of sorrow of separation and yearning for union that pervades the outpourings of all the mystic poets of India.

APPAR

APPAR (TIRUNAVUKKARASU) (7th Century A.D.)

Appar or Tirunavukkarasu was one of the four famous Saivite saints, known as *Nālwar,* the other three being Sundarar, Tirujnanasambandhar and Manikkavachakar.

The name Appar was affectionately conferred on him by Sambandhar when they first met.

Appar's devotion to God was that of a servant, while Sundarar treated God like a friend, Manikkavachakar like a lover and Sambandhar like a father. Appar was born in 600 A.D. in Tiruvamur, a village in the south Arcot district of Tamil Nadu.

A series of family tragedies created a "*dark night of the soul*" for Appar, who turned to religious studies, social work, philanthropy and even conversion to Jainism, in an attempt to get mental peace, which still eluded him.

Appar's sister, firmly rooted in her devotion to Lord Siva, brought back the religious prodigy suffering from severe stomach pain to a Siva temple, where the repentant Appar prayed, got relieved of his pain and became an ardent devotee of Lord Siva and went from temple to temple singing the praises of the Lord.

Appar's songs of devotion, over 3000 in number, constitute the 4th, 5th and 6th parts of *Tirumurai*, Saivite canonical literature, *Tevāram* (Garland to God), the first three parts being the songs of Sambandhar.

Appar lived upto the age of 81 years and died at *Tiruppugalur.*

AVVAIYAR

AVVAIYAR (7th Century A.D.)

Avvaiyar, "*the grandmother of Tamil literature*", as she is affectionately called, was one of the greatest singer saints of ancient India.

Myth and legend have covered in mist the biographical details of Avvaiyar's life.

Many believe that there were more than one Avvaiyar. She could have been born any time during the period 3rd century B.C. to 7th century A.D.

There is a statue of Avvaiyar on the Marina beach in Chennai (India) under which her birth date is mentioned as 1st century B.C.

But the Avvaiyar who has authored *Vināyakar Akaval,* was more probably a contemporary of the Saivite saint Sundarar, who probably lived in the 7th or 8th century A.D.

Avvaiyar was a great devotee of Lord Gaṇeśa and is considered the pioneer saint who propagated worship of Gaṇeśa in South India.

Avvaiyar's *Vināyakar Akaval* is a veritable treasurehouse of devotion through the Yogic path.

TIRUJNANASAMBANDHAR

TIRUJNANASAMBANDHAR (7th Century A.D.)

Tirujnanasambandhar is the infant prodigy among the mystic saints of India. He lived only for a short period of 16 years, but during his short life he demonstrated an intensity of spiritual illumination and God-intoxication attained by very few other saints.

Tirujnanasambandhar was born in *Sirkazhi*, a place near Kumbhakonam, in Tanjavur district of Tamil Nadu, India. He received his spiritual illumination miraculously at the tender age of three and thereafter there was no stopping him from visiting the various temples, singing devotional hymns to his chosen Deity: Lord Siva, the Auspicious One, and performing miracles wherever he went.

Tirujnanasambandhar has composed 383 hymns in which he sang of the temples he visited and the glory and grace of God. This mystic saint's approach to God is like that of a son to his father. These hymns are known as *Tévaarams* or garlands for God.

Among the temples visited by Tirujnanasambandhar are: *Tirumaraikkadu*, where along with Appar, another famous elderly Saivite saint, by devotional songs, he got the temple door opened and closed, *Tirunallar, Madurai* (where he brought the King back to Saivite faith (from Jainism)), *Tiruvannamalai, Tiruvaazhangaadu, Kalahasti, Mylapore, Chidambaram* and *Rameswaram.*

The songs of Tirujnanasambandhar reveal a filial proximity to God. He appeals to God to bestow grace and work miracles so that His omnipotence is established and righteousness triumphs.

ANDAL

ANDAL (7th Century A.D.)

Andal's songs are imbued with bridal mysticism. Her life-history is misty with legends and myths. She was supposed to be discovered as an infant lying under a Tulsi (Basil) plant by the temple priest, Perialwar, also known as *Vishnuchitta.* Her birth date has been assigned by modern scholars to the middle of 7th century A.D.

The Vishnu temple at *Srivilliputtur* (some sixty kilometres from the modern city of *Madurai*) was where Andal developed her bridal devotion. Daily she would deck herself with flower garlands and imagine herself to be the bride of *Krishna* who sported with *Gopis* in *Gokula* on the banks of the Yamuna river.

She deemed herself to be a Gopi, rising early in the morning, waking her companions from sleep, having a ritualistic bath and going to *Nandagopa's* residence to pay homage to *Krishna.* This imagery is the central theme of *Tiruppāvai,* a string of 30 songs.

Legend has it that Andal was taken in bridal attire to Sri Ranganatha's temple at Srirangam, where she entered the *sanctum sanctorum* and got merged with the Lord.

The temple at Srivilliputtur today houses the images of Ranganatha and Andal, as the Lord and His spouse, where thousands throng to worship, especially during the month of Margasirsa (December 15 to January 15).

Recitation of Andal's 30 songs of *Tiruppāvai* is resorted to by women of South India during this period.

TIRUMANGAI AZHWAR

TIRUMANGAI AZHWAR (8th Century A.D.)

Tirumangai Azhwar, one of the more important among the twelve Azhwars, was born in a village in Tamilnad, called *Tirukuraiyular*, in a non-Brahmin family.

He was a hero well trained in the martial arts and the Chola King conferred the title *Parakala* on him and gave him a small territory to rule. He hence came to be called *Tirumangai Mannan*. He had also another name: *Kaliyān*.

A woman named Kumudavalli, who married him, got him converted to Vaishnavism and compelled him to feed a thousand people every day. Unable to meet the heavy expenses involved in the daily feeding of a thousand persons, Tirumangai resorted to highway robbery.

Legend has it that in one of the highway robberies, the Lord cast a spell on him and spiritually transformed him, by teaching him the sacred mantra: *NAMONARAYANAYA*.

The reformed devotee burst into songs, repenting for his errant past and expressing his deep love for the Lord of his heart. He was a prolific poet. Of the 4000 verses in the *Nālayira Divyaprabandham*, the compendium of poems by the 12 Azhwars, 1250 verses are the contribution of Tirumangai Azhwar.

His most important work is called *Periya Tirumozhi*. He has composed 5 more works.

In his songs, he expresses his mystical devotion to God. Tirumangai Azhwar has extolled the deities in 40 temples scattered throughout India, from *Badrinath* in the North to *Tirukkurungudi* in the South.

SANKARACHARYA

SANKARACHARYA (788-820 A.D.)

Adi Sankara, the Nambudiri Brahmin from Kerala, who lived for only 32 years, was one of the greatest sons of India. He was a philosopher, poet and a mystic saint.

His literary and intellectual output was prolific. He wrote commentaries for the three works which form the cornerstone of Hinduism: The *Upanishads*, the *Bhagavat Geeta* and the *Brahmasutras*. He composed several beautiful devotional hymns like the *Saundaryalahari* and *Sivanandalahari* and great philosophical treatises like the *Vivekachoodaamani*.

He reduced the thousands of religious cults and sects to six broad modes of worship, called *Shanmata*: *Saiva*, *Saakta*, *Saurya*, *Vaishnava*, *Kaumara* and *Gaanapatya*.

He established five mutts in the distant corners of India to strengthen the unity and integrity of the country: at Badrinath in the Himalayas, at Puri in the east, Dwaraka in the west and at Sringeri and Kanchi in the south.

Most important of all, he propounded the philosophy of *Advaita* as a panacea for the ills of the world. Sankara stated the essence of Advaita in just half a verse: *Brahma Satyam, Jagat Mithya, Jeevo Brahmaiva Naaparah*, meaning: The Supreme (Brahman) is the only reality, the phenomenal world is an illusion, the individual soul is the same as the Supreme Spirit, not different.

The essence of Sankara's teaching is: All that exists—seen and unseen—is in reality One and not two. All life is One, nondual and non-multiple. There is a spark of the divine in every unit of creation. In this view there is no need for hatred or confrontation on the basis of sex, religion, caste, nationality, race, colour or economic condition.

Sankara's teaching is the way to break down the barriers, the walls and the fences that divide our world. No wonder he is called *Jagat Guru*, the world teacher.

Though Sankara emphasised that knowledge of the identity of the soul with the Supreme was the ultimate means to liberation, he also felt the necessity for devotion to break down the ego and lead to knowledge.

And since devotion necessitated a personal God with attributes (*Saguna Brahman*), he advised people to worship God in six forms (Shanmata), i.e. God visualised as Siva, Sakti, Sun, Vishnu, Kumara or Subrahmanya and as Ganapati.

To facilitate the process of devotion, Sankara composed several beautiful devotional hymns, brimming with poetic ecstasy.

These devotional hymns of Sankara are sung by millions of devotees in India, in temple precincts and worship corners in individual homes regularly at dawn and dusk.

SUNDARAR

SUNDARAR (8th-9th Century A.D.)

Sundarar was one of the four most famous Saivite mystics (popularly known in Tamil as *Naalwar*), the other three being *Tirujnana Sambandhar, Appar* (also known as *Tirunāvukkarasar*) and *Mānikkavachakar.*

Ramana Maharishi used to say: "The devotion of Sundarar to the Lord is that of a friend, of Manikkavachakar that of the beloved, of Appar that of a servant and Sambandhar that of a son."

It is difficult to separate the scanty biographical details about Sundarar (also known as Sundaramurthy) from the myths and legends connected with his life.

He presumably lived during late 8th-early 9th century A.D. He was born in the village of Tirunavalur, now known as Tirunamanallur, about 11 miles west of *Panrutti* Railway Station in Tamil Nadu.

Realising, in a revelation, that the best form of worship of God was to sing His praises, Sundarar composed songs, known as *Tevaarams* (lit. garlands for God), 38000 of them, but only a hundred are now available.

Sundarar went around, visiting the various temples of South India and composing songs in praise of the Deities in them. He was a friend of the Kerala Ruler, Cheraman and visited Tiruvanchikkulam temple near Kodungalloor.

Sundarar sang of the glory of his friend, God, who was both immanent and transcendent, and by whose grace one could attain both *bhukti* and *mukti,* enjoyment and liberation.

KAMBAN

KAMBAN (9th Century A.D.)

Kamban, the Tamil poet who was the first to write the epic *Ramayana* in a regional language, is the pride of Tamil Nadu and Tamil language.

Subramania Bharati eulogises Kamban by saying "*Tamilnadu is the state where Kamban was born*".

Kamban's deep devotion to God, incarnate as Lord Rama, pervades every stanza in *Kamba Ramayana,* a work comprising 11000 stanzas.

It is claimed that the devotional lyrics of the *Alwars* had a profound influence on Kamban.

Biographical details about Kamban are scanty. He is believed to have been born the son of a weaver named Adityan.

Tiruvazhundur in Tanjavur district of Tamil Nadu has been mentioned as the birthplace of Kamban.

The name *Kamban* is unique, presumably it is derived from the Tamil word for a pillar, near which he was discovered by the Chola King.

Kamban is called *Kavi Chakravarti,* "the Emperor among poets". Kamban's poetry, rich in lyrical quality and conceptual grandeur, has been compared to that of Keats, Swinburne and Milton.

He is the Tamil equivalent of the Hindi poet Tulsidas.

The literary embellishments in Kamban's songs achieve greatness, because of his deep devotion to God, whom he saw as Rama, the Supreme Saviour.

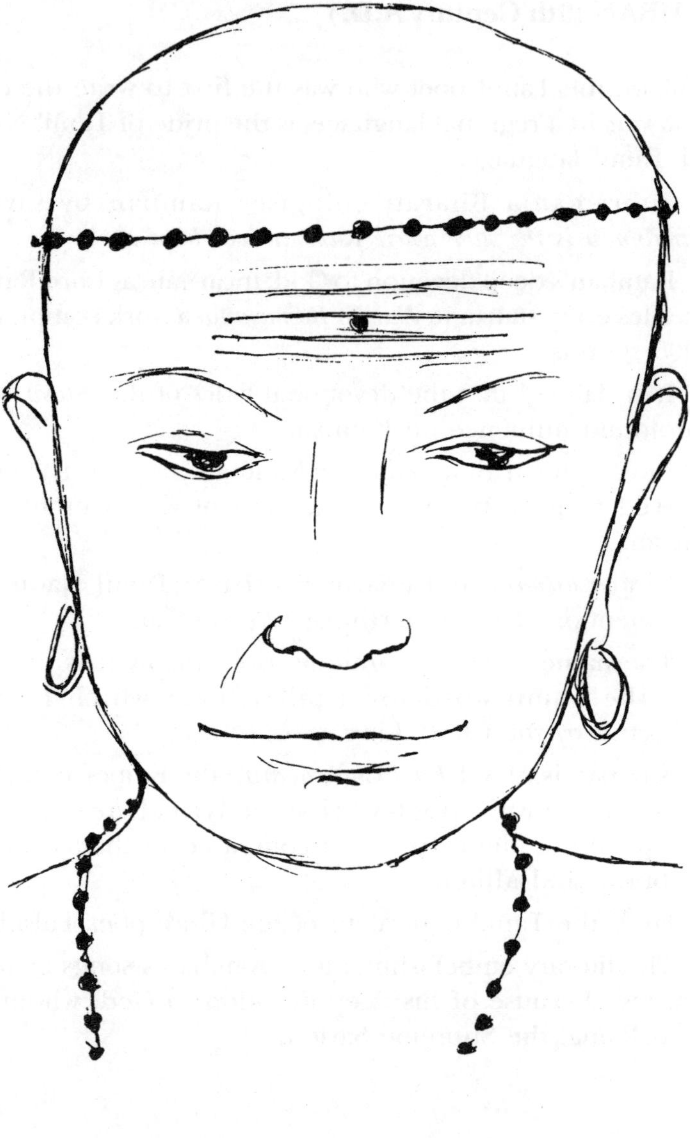

MANIKKAVACHAKAR

MANIKKAVACHAKAR (9th Century A.D.)

The songs of Manikkavachakar, the Saivite saint, who is believed to have lived in the 9th century A.D., are imbued with bridal mysticism, like the songs of Andal, the Vaishnavite saint of the 7th century.

Manikkavachakar was born in *Tiruvadavur,* a place near Madurai, the Pandyan capital and his original name was *Tiruvadavurar.* He was devoted to Lord Siva from childhood and poured forth his devotion in mellifluous poetry and acquired the title of *Manikkavachakar* (lit.: "He whose words are rubies").

This South Indian saint has been compared to St. Augustine, St. Paul and St. Francis of Assissi.

The Lord was the object of his love and he deemed himself as the separated lover yearning for union with his love. Manikkavachakar's major works are the *Tiruvāchakam* and *Tirukkovaiyar,* the first comprising 656 verses and the latter 400 verses.

Among the various places of pilgrimage visited by Manikkavachakar, three temples are most important. These are the temple of *Tirupperundurai,** where he first perceived God as his teacher and composed the famous hymn: *Tiruppalliyezhucchi,* the temple of *Tiruvannamalai,* where he composed the *Tiruvembavai,* eulogising group worship by young girls during the month of Mārgasirsa (mid December to mid January), and the famous temple of *Chidambaram,* where he composed the *Tiruvāchakam* and attained salvation.

The thirty songs of Manikkavachakar comprising the *Tiruvembavai* (20 songs) and *Tiruppalliyezhucchi* (10 songs) reveal intense devotion to God and self-surrender. In the eloquent words of Rev. G.U. Pope, "*South India needed a personal God, an assurance of immortality and a call to prayer. These it found in Manikkavachakar's compositions.*"

*While the location of *Tiruvannamalai* and *Chidambaram* are well known, not many know where *Tirupperundurai* is located. This is because it is now known as *Aavudaiyaar Koil.* The location is in the *Arantaangi* taluq of Tanjavur district in Tamil Nadu. It is nine miles by road from Arantaangi railway station on the *Tiruvarur-Karaikudi* rail line. One can also drive from *Kāraikkudi.*

NAMMALWAR

NAMMALWAR (880-930 A.D.)

Nammalwar was one of the greatest Vaishnavite saints (called *Alwars*). Literally the term *Alwar* means one who dives into the Divine or is God-intoxicated.

The hymns of the *Alwars,* 4000 in number, were collected by a sage called Nathamuni in one volume called *Divya Prabandham.* Nammalwar's major work *Tiruvāimozhi* constitutes the third thousand in *Divya Prabandham.* His three other poems *Tiruvrittam, Tiruvāsiriyam* and *Periyatiruvantādi* are included in the fourth thousand of the compendium, also known as *Nālāyira Prabandham.*

Biographical details about Nammalwar are scanty and mixed up with mythical legends. It is however accepted that he was born in Alwar Tirunagari in Tirunelveli district of Tamil Nadu.

Sri Krishna was the incarnation of God, which appealed most to Nammalwar and his approach to God was one of bridal mysticism.

The soul is the bride of God and is drawn towards union with the Lord, incarnate as the Eternal Lover of captivating charm, Sri Krishna.

In his songs, Nammalwar pours out his longing for union with the Divine. They are soaked in mystical experience and deal with the five vital tenets of Vaishnavism (*Arthapanchak*): *Glory of God, nature of the soul, the goal of life, the means of achieving it* and *the obstacles to be overcome.*

Nammalwar lived only for a short period of 35 years. But his impress on Vaishnavism was lasting. The concept of *Saranāgadi* or total surrender to God was his indelible contribution.

DEVARA DASIMAYYA

DEVARA DASIMAYYA (10th Century A.D.)

Devara Dasimayya is the pioneer propagator of the *Veera Saivite* spiritual tradition, whose later luminaries include such stalwarts as Basavanna, Mahadevi Akka and Allama Prabhu.

Veera Saivism was a movement devoted to the worship of God as Siva and rejected social inequalities.

Devara Dasimayya was born in the village of *Mudanduru* in Karnataka in the tenth century A.D.

The village had a temple dedicated to Siva, as *Rāmanātha,* Siva as worshipped by Rama.

All songs of Devara Dasimayya are addressed to Ramanatha.

Convinced that working in the world was part of worship of the Lord and a means to realise Him, Dasimayya became a weaver. He married *Duggale,* who was a devoted wife to him.

Dasimayya was a vigorous proponent of Saivism.

The King in whose kingdom he lived was a Chalukyan ruler, named Jayasimha, who was a follower of Jainism.

Legend has it that Devara Dasimayya converted the King to Saivism through a series of miracles.

As a result of his passionate espousal of Saivism, people of all beliefs, jungle tribes and Brahmins, became his followers.

He laid emphasis on faith, devotion and surrender to God.

There is a story that when he wanted to give up the world, Dasimayya went to his native village, Mudanduru and told the Deity in the temple, Ramanatha: "I've lived my life and now you must return me to yourself."

The Lord obliged and both Dasimayya and his wife joined the Infinite.

PATTINATTAR

PATTINATTAR (10th Century A.D.)

Pattinattar is one of the most famous Tamil Saivite saints.

His songs pouring out his devotion to Lord Siva also convey his contempt for the illusory world of material riches, egoism and vanity.

His original name was *Tiruvenkadavar.* He was a wealthy man living with his wife Sivakala in Kaveripoompattinam, in the Chola kingdom. How he gave up all his earthly possessions and became a mendicant is an interesting story.

He adopted a son named Marutappan, who, returning from an overseas trade journey, gave Pattinattar a box containing some broken needles and an inscription on paper which read: "Even these broken needles will not follow you!" The transience and unreality of earthly possessions dawned on Pattinattar who gave up all his wealth and became a wandering recluse.

He visited all the Siva temples in the South of India, including Chidambaram, Kalahasti and Kanchipuram, and sang inspiring songs, pouring out his devotion to God.

Many miracles are attributed to Pattinattar, including the revival of a dead man and burning the corpse of his mother with plantain stems.

Pattinattar is believed to have attained lasting samadhi in *Tiruvottiyoor.*

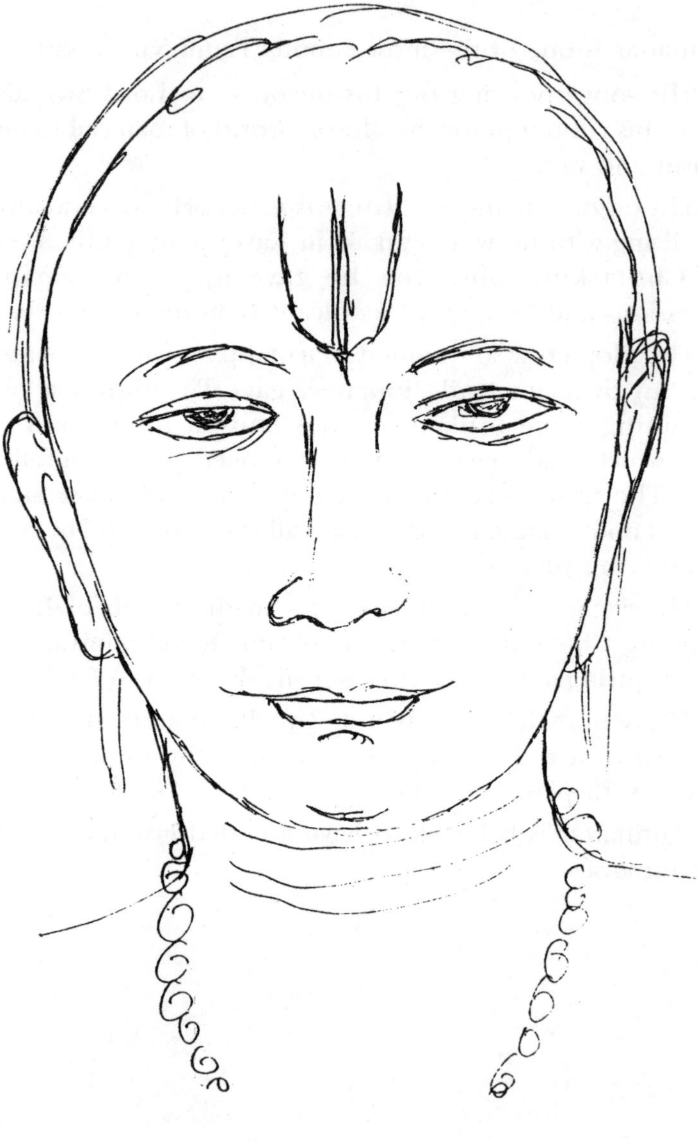

RAMANUJA

RAMANUJA (1017-1137 A.D.)

Ramanuja, the Vaishnavite saint, was unique in many ways.

He broke the barriers of caste. He allowed untouchables into temples. He even allowed a Muslim devotee to worship in the temples. He shared the sacred mantra "*Om Namo Narayanaya*" with the common people.

Born in 1017 A.D. at Sri Perumbudur, 25 miles from Chennai, Ramanuja lived a rich and full life for 120 years, living about 60 years in the holy Srirangam temple.

He preached his philosophy of *Visishta Advaita*, according to which God is the Ruler and Lord of the universe. *Jiva* or the individual soul is God's servant and worshipper and as such should surrender completely to God to win His grace.

Of course, to Ramanuja and all Vaishnavites, God exists as Lord Narayana or Vishnu and should be worshipped as such.

Ramanuja wrote several works like *Vedanta Samgraha, Sri Bhashya, Gita Bhashya, Vedanta Dipa, Saranagati Gadya, Sri Ranga Gadya, Sri Vaikuntha Gadya* and *Nithyagrantha.*

Ramanuja travelled throughout India, preaching the path of devotion or *Bhakti Marga.* He visited Kashi, Kashmir, Badrinath, Tirupati, Mysore, etc.

Ramanuja died in 1137 A.D. By the time of his death, he had converted millions to the path of devotion to God.

Ramanuja's adoration of God in the manifestation dear to his heart was intense as can be seen from the prayers in his various *Gadyas.*

JAYADEVA

JAYADEVA (12th Century A.D.)

Few scholars dispute the fact that Jayadeva, the Orissan poet, lived in the 12th century. He was a Sanskrit scholar and poet. A Brahmin by birth, he married Padmavati, a dancer. She danced to his songs.

Jayadeva's masterpiece is the *Gita Govinda,* a poem extolling the love of Radha and Krishna, in erotic imagery.

There are 24 songs in *Gita Govinda.* They are called *Ashtapadis,* since each song contains eight stanzas.

The terse beauty of the Sanskrit language, made melodious use of by Jayadeva, invests these songs with musical magic.

These songs inspired Sri Krishna Chaitanya, the great Vaishnavite saint of Bengal. They also inspired the artists of Jammu and Kashmir to evolve a new style of painting called the *Basohli* school of painting.

In the Krishna temple of Guruvayoor in Kerala, Jayadeva's songs are sung daily, set to music in Carnatic ragas.

In Nepal, they are sung during spring celebrations.

The *Gita Govinda* of Jayadeva is known as the Indian Song of songs. Sir Edwin Arnold who was one of the first to translate it into English called it *The Song Celestial.*

Two of Jayadeva's songs have been included by Guru Arjan Dev in the Adi Guru Grantha, the holy scripture of the Sikhs.

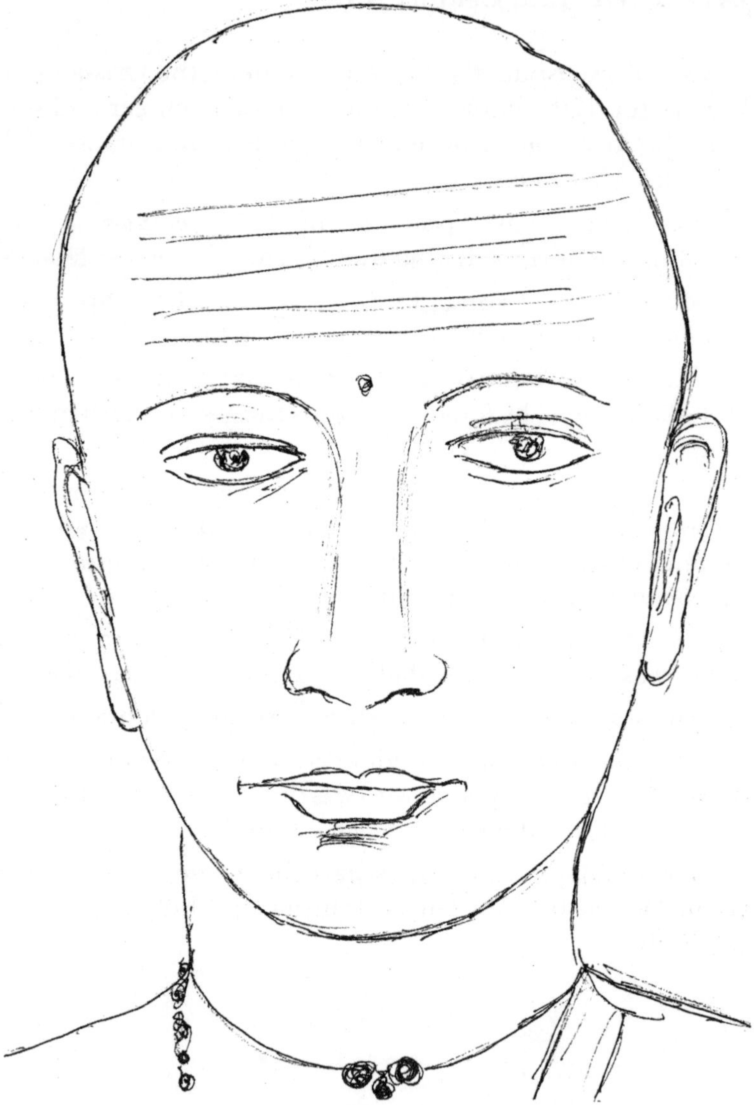

BASAVANNA

BASAVANNA (1106-1167 A.D.)

Basavanna is the great religious leader of Karnataka who established *Veerasaivism*, a movement devoted to the worship of Siva, which rejected inequality of every kind, rituals and caste taboos and exalted work in the world in the name of God.

The songs of Basavanna, commonly known as *Vachanas*, reflect not only his passionate love of Siva, the Auspicious Lord, but also his deep-felt views on the maladies which afflicted the society in which he lived.

Basavanna was born in 1106 A.D. and died in 1167 or 1168 A.D. Born in a place called *Manigavalli*, he was brought up by foster parents (his own parents having died early) at *Bagevadi*. At the age of sixteen, he left home, finding the caste system and the ritualism of his home stifling and reached *Kappadisangama*, where three rivers meet.

The Lord of the Meeting Rivers, *Kudalasangamadeva*, becomes his *Ishtadevata* or Chosen Deity and every song of his, he addresses to Him.

Following a revelation from the Lord, Basavanna went to *Kalyana* and became a minister of King Bijjala. Using his political and financial power, he sought to create an egalitarian society, devoted to the worship of Siva.

Great saints like Allama Prabhu and Mahadevi Akka became active members of this community, preaching the breakdown of barriers based on caste, class, sex, orthodoxy, social convention and religious ritual.

Basavanna preached and practised love of God and love of man.

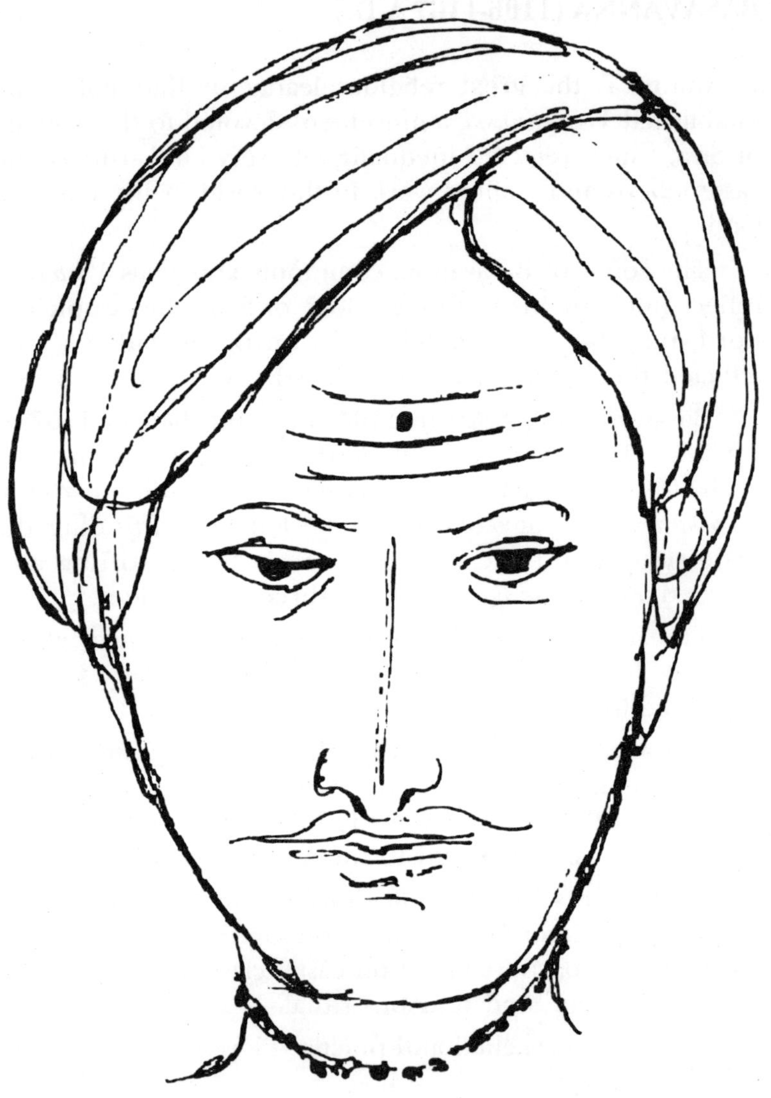

ALLAMA PRABHU

ALLAMA PRABHU (12th Century A.D.)

Allama Prabhu, along with Basavanna and Mahadevi Akka, may be considered the pioneer of *Veerasaivism*, a movement devoted to the worship of Siva, preaching the breakdown of social barriers, established conventions and external rituals. Love of God and love of man are the central doctrines of *Veerasaivism.*

Biographical details about Allama Prabhu are scanty and get blurred by legendary beliefs.

But there is no doubt about his birth in the 12th century, in Karnataka, India and his being a contemporary of Basavanna and Mahadevi Akka, both of whom lived in the 12th century.

The premature death of Allama's wife, *Kamalate* and the consequent grief made Allama wander and end up in a cave temple where the saint *Animisayya* gave him a *Linga* (Lord's idol) and instantly Allama became spiritually enlightened.

Out of his mystical experience, Allama sang the glory of God, as one who manifested Himself as the Lord of the cave temple. He composed 1321 hymns, which cover the whole gamut of spiritual progress from devotion to refuge to ultimate union with God.

Allama Prabhu rejected the acquisition of occult powers or *Siddhis* as impediments to liberation for the spiritual aspirant.

Allama was the undisputed master of the Veerasaivite movement.

While Basava was termed *Anna* or the brother, and Mahadevi as *Akka* or sister, Allama was called *Prabhu* or Master to everyone.

MAHADEVI AKKA

MAHADEVI AKKA (12th Century A.D.)

Mahadevi Akka, the fiery Kannada Veera-Saivite saint, was born in *Udutadi*, a village in Sivamogga, Karnataka, India. From the age of ten, when she was initiated into spirituality, till her death in her early twenties, she wandered, God-intoxicated, seeking union with her Beloved Lord Siva, the Lord "white as jasmine" (*Mallikarjuna*).

She poured out her love for God in passionate poetry. The bridal mysticism of Mahadevi Akka is more intense than that of Andal, the Vaishnavite saint who lived in the 7th century A.D.

Though the Deity in the temple at Udutadi, her birthplace, was known as *Mallikarjuna*, it is probably the deity in the temple at Sri Sailam (in Andhra Pradesh), where she ultimately retired and attained salvation, famously known as Mallikarjuna, that she refers to as her beloved in each of her songs.

Mahadevi Akka broke all social shackles, by discarding all clothing and covering herself only in her tresses of hair. Other Veera-Saivite saints like Allama Prabhu recognised the saint in her and accepted her in their company.

Mahadevi Akka expresses her love for God in the three traditional forms of love: forbidden love, love in separation and love in union. This is not very different from the way *Meera*, the Rajasthani princess of the 15th-16th century, expressed her love for her Lover: Sri Krishna.

Andal, Mahadevi Akka and *Meera* can be considered the Trinity of women-mystic saints of India, whose bridal mysticism produced great devotional poetry.

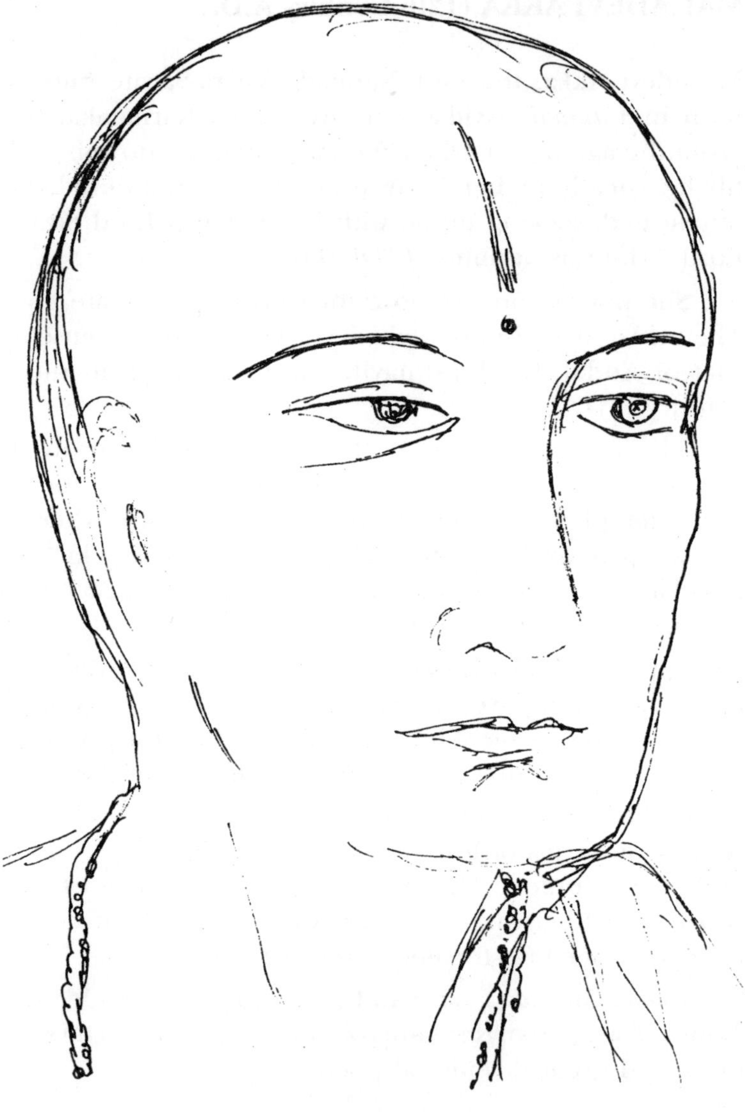

MADHVACHARYA

MADHVACHARYA (1199-1278 A.D.)

Madhvacharya, along with Sankara and Ramanuja, forms the Trinity of Vedantic philosophers.

While Sankara propounded *Advaita,* Ramanuja *Visishtadvaita,* Madhva advocated *Dvaita.*

All the three held God or *Brahman* as the only transcendent reality who was also immanent.

The difference was that while Sankara held the phenomenal world to be *Māyā* or illusion, and the individual soul to be identical with Brahman or God, both *Madhvacharya* and *Ramanuja* stressed that matter and souls were real, but dependent on God.

Madhvacharya held that ignorance was the cause of the soul's bondage. He, like *Ramanuja,* felt that devotion to a personal God like *Vishnu* was the way to liberation and release from ignorance.

Even *Advaitins* hold that Divine Grace is required for achieving self-realization. But Madhva went one step further and said that divine grace should be earned by surrender and devotion.

Madhva was born in a village near Udupi in 1199 A.D. He became learned in Vedic lore even at a very early age and became a *Sanyāsin* (celibate recluse). Dissatisfied with Sankara's philosophy, he developed his own, to which many were attracted, including his own teacher *Achyuta Prakasha.* Madhvacharya founded the famous Krishna temple at Udupi, which became a centre for his followers.

He authored 37 works, the more important being his commentaries on *Brahmasutra* and *Bhagavat Gita* and a work delineating the meaning of *Mahābhārata.*

He died in 1278 A.D. at the age of 79.

"Ekam Sat. Vipraah bahudha vadanti" (The reality is One. Learned Ones describe it diversely) goes the Vedic Chant. Madhva's philosophy has to be viewed in this light.

VEDANTA DESIKAN

VEDANTA DESIKAN (1268-1369 A.D.)

Vedanta Desikan, the renowned Vaishnavite saint, may be deemed the *St. Paul of the Vaishnavite movement.*

He propagated the teachings of Sri Ramanuja, the Pioneer of Vaishnavism, with vigour and passion.

He was a many-sided genius: poet, philosopher, saint and debator.

Vedanta Desikan was born in September, 1268 at *Toopul,* a suburb of Kanchipuram.

By the age of twenty, he mastered all religious scriptures.

He married and became a householder.

Spending his days in Tiruvahindrapuram, Satyamangalam, Kanchipuram and Srirangam, from 1290 to 1369, Vedanta Desikan composed several works, important among them being *Stotra Ratna Mala,* comprising 32 devotional hymns, the most famous being *Pādukasahasra, Subhasitanivi, Yadavabhyudaya, Hamsasandesa,* etc.

Vedanta Desikan died in Srirangam in 1369.

The devotional songs of Vedanta Desikan are illustrative of his innate love of God, his utter surrender to the Divine will and total self-abnegation.

NAMDEV

NAMDEV (1270-1350 A.D.)

Namdev is not only the foremost mystic saint-poet of Maharashtra but one of the best known in India.

Born the son of a tailor in 1270 A.D., he spent most of his life at Pandharpur living in communion with Lord Panduranga. Namdev was a contemporary of the other famous mystic saint of Maharashtra, Jnaneswar. Namdev was five years older than Jnaneswar, but unlike Jnaneswar who lived only for a short period of 22 years, Namdev lived upto the ripe old age of 80 years.

The two saints travelled together all over North India, singing Bhajans.

Namdev's songs (called *Abhangs* in Marathi) are soaked in devotion to God. They express the intense yearning of the devotee for a vision of God as also the fulfilling bliss which results from God-realisation.

61 of his songs are included in the Granth Sahib, the holy book of the Sikhs.

While Jnaneswar's mystic experience was blended with spiritual knowledge (*Jnana*), Namdev's was one of total devotion.

It was Namdev's view that repetition of God's name resulted in the removal of duality and led to the Advaitic goal of union with the Supreme Power.

Though Namdev was married and had five children (four sons and a daughter), his obsession with the Lord of Pandharpur left him no time to attend to family matters.

Namdev may be deemed the pioneer of the Bhakti movement, which later spread to the north and attracted such stalwarts as Kabir, Tulsidas and Surdas.

The philosophic school founded by Namdev is known as *Varakari Sampradaya.*

Namdev's devotional songs are sung with love and devotion all over Maharashtra even today.

JNANESWAR

JNANESWAR (1275-1296 A.D.)

Jnaneswar was the famous mystic philosopher-poet-saint of Maharashtra, who, despite a short life of 22 years, has bequeathed a legacy of immortal works that remains an inspiration to the people of Maharashtra to this day.

His three important works are: *Jnāneswari*, a monumental yet simple commentary on the Bhagavat Gita, *Anubhavamrita*, in which he explains his philosophy of life and *Abhangs* or devotional lyrics.

Jnaneswar may be considered the philosophic founder of the *Bhakti movement in Maharashtra*, of which other luminaries are: Namdev (a contemporary of Jnaneswar), Eknath and Tukaram. Jnaneswar's ideal of Bhakti is unique. It is not merely a subjective feeling, but the heart of reality, the *summum bonum* of life. Bhakti or God-devotion or God-intoxication is the root of all moral qualities.

Jnaneswar saw no conflict between Bhakti and the concept of Advaita.

The universe is, according to Jnaneswar, an expression of God's love for Himself.

As water sports with itself in the form of waves, the *Ātman* or the Universal Soul plays with itself in the form of the universe and feels happy. God has become man to experience His own affection. *One need not forsake the world to find God.*

Human life is a precious gift of God. It should be kept pure and holy. The summit of all virtues is God-devotion. There is no object of love greater than God.

In the pathway of loving devotion, the organs of the senses and the tempers of the mind are turned towards God and become vehicles of His love.

According to Jnaneswar, the God-intoxicated become like moons without spots and suns without the scorching heat. Jnaneswar's religion of love is a unique contribution to mankind.

LAL DED

LAL DED (14th Century A.D.)

Lal Ded was the most famous poet-saint of Kashmir. Biographical details about her are scanty.

She is believed to have been born in a village a few miles southeast of Srinagar about 1335 A.D.

She was married at the age of twelve, ill-treated by her mother-in-law and left home to be a recluse, living in jungles and mountain caves.

Lal Ded was basically a Saivite Yogin, God-intoxicated and passionately seeking God-realisation in this very life. She did not believe in liberation after death. A true devotee of Siva had to be a *Jeevanmukta*, liberated, while alive.

According to Lalla, the body itself is the abode of the Lord and hence we must direct our gaze within and not seek Him outside. The body must be regarded as the temple for the worship of God. Worldly life is no bar to liberation. Life is not to be renounced, but transformed. Renunciation of worldly life is escapism and cowardice. Only ego, the cause of all troubles, should be given up. Constant awareness of the Self is meditation.

The songs of Lal Ded or Lalla Yogeswari, commonly known as *vaaks*, express in beautiful imagery and exquisite Kashmiri poetry her intense Bhakti or devotion to God, who is immanent and omnipresent.

Lal Ded died between 1388 A.D. and 1391 A.D.

Sheikh Nur-ud-din Wali, a Muslim saint, said of her: "That Lalla of Padmanpur—she drank her fill of divine nectar. She was indeed an *Avatāra.*"

BILWA MANGAL

BILWA MANGAL (14th Century A.D.)

Bilwa Mangal, the author of the famous *Krishnakarnamritam*, dealing with the charming exploits of Krishna, was also known as *Lilasuka*. He was born in Kerala, South India, near Parur, in the late 13th-early 14th century A.D.

Bilwa Mangal was originally infatuated with a courtesan named *Chintāmani*, who one day chided him: "If only you have one thousandth of the love you have for me for God, how much better it would be for you!" On hearing these words, a sudden transformation took place in his life. The dissolute one became a great devotee of Lord Krishna and poured out his love and devotion in the inimitable poem, *Krishnakarnamritam*, which won plaudits from the great Vaishnavite saint Chaitanya Mahaprabhu, who obtained a copy of it during his visit to Tiruvananthapuram and wrote a commentary on it. He remarked: "I treasure *Sri Krishna Karnamrita* as the very jewel that decorates my heart."

The mellifluous Sanskrit of Bilwa Mangal, mingled with the ecstatic love and devotion he bears to his chosen Deity, Sri Krishna, invests these songs with a quality so rare that when sung, they are, as the title indicates, nectar to the ears of all listeners.

Bilwa Mangal is believed to have lived upto a ripe old age of eighty years.

JANA BAI

JANA BAI (14th Century A.D.)

Jana Bai, the Maharashtra poet saint, ranks among the foremost women saints of India.

Her devotional songs reveal her total love for God, who appeared to her as the Deity in the temple at Pandharpur, Vittala.

Jana Bai was born of a low caste family and was sent to work as a servant in the house of a tailor named *Damasheti* who was the father of the great saint Namdev.

As Jana Bai grew, she came under the influence of Namdev and other saints of Maharashtra who frequented Namdev's house.

While she carried out her household duties, Jana Bai sang of the glory of her beloved Vittala and felt His presence in and around her.

In one of her ecstatic outbursts, she sang: "I eat God, I sleep in God, I breathe God, I feel God, speak God and I give God and take God."

Jana Bai spent her life at Pandharpur, in the company of saints who flocked to Pandharpur from all parts of India, all the time singing of her communion with God.

Children recite Jana Bai's songs even today.

She herself was a child in her love for and devotion and service to God.

VIDYAPATI

VIDYAPATI (1350-1460 A.D.)

Vidyapati, the court poet of Mithila, during the reign of Raja Shivasimha was born in *Bisapi,* a village in Mithila.

He received his education from *Harimishra,* a reputed scholar.

Vidyapati's poetic genius attracted everyone, including the ruler *Shivasimha* and his queen *Lakhima Devi.*

Vidyapati was a contemporary of Chandidas, the Bengali poet whose approach to religion and poetry was similar to that of Vidyapati.

Vidyapati's songs are full of erotic imagery, like Jayadeva's but also soaked in devotion amd melodious grace.

Vidyapati wrote his first poem when he was hardly 20 years old. His major work is *Padāvali,* a collection of hundreds of his poems, covering his entire life period.

His poetic obsession was the love of Radha and Krishna, the divine couple and he has dealt with it with elegance, simplicity, sentiment and sensuousness.

The eager longing to meet, the bliss of union and the sadness of separation of the lovers are all dealt with passion and sincerity.

The songs of Vidyapati are even now sung daily by the women of Mithila.

SANT RAIDAS

SANT RAIDAS (1500-1576 A.D.)

Raidas, also known as Ravidas, the great mystic poet-saint, was a contemporary of Meera and Kabir.

Biographical details are scanty and often contradictory.

He is believed to have been born of cobbler caste in a village near Varanasi.

Like Kabir, he was a disciple of Saint Ramanand, and like Kabir, he had no academic training.

His outburst of songs was purely the result of his inner experience.

Sant Raidas preached pure devotion to God and he himself practised what he preached.

Varanasi was the stronghold of upper caste Brahmins, who were opposed to any lower caste devotee becoming prominent.

But Raidas's singleminded devotion to God won him friends and admirers and followers from near and far.

Meera of Rajasthan became his disciple and invited him to Chittor.

Sant Raidas travelled to various pilgrim centres like *Mathura, Brindavan, Haridwar* and even *Tirupati.*

He is believed to have died at Varanasi in 1576 A.D. Raidas's deeply devotional songs have had a great influence on Hindi literature. 41 of his songs have been included in the Granth Sahib of the Sikhs.

Like Kanakadasa, Raidas was also a critic of the caste system. Like him, he also felt that there was no place for caste distinctions in the realm of spirituality and devotion to God.

He considered human life as a wonderful opportunity for God-realisation.

He laid more emphasis on inner prayer and less on external rituals of worship.

He poured out his devotion to his favourite Deity Lord Rama in moving songs that, in the words of Sheela Devi, "*opened the floodgates of bhakti in the realm of Indian poetry.*"

NARSI MEHTA

NARSI MEHTA (1414-1480 A.D.)

Narsi Mehta is the foremost poet-saint of Gujarat.

His songs reveal an intense devotion to Lord Krishna, his chosen *Ishtadevata* (Favourite Deity).

Narsi Mehta's songs, simple and moving and soaked in the basic philosophy of the Bhakti cult, have become part of the folk tradition of Gujarat.

All his life, Narsi Mehta preached humility, equal compassion for all beings, self-discipline and total devotion to Lord Krishna.

He disregarded caste barriers and social restrictions. He deemed all human beings as children of God, *Harijan*.

He was born at Talaja, a village near Junagadh in Saurashtra, Gujarat. He lost his father at the age of three and his mother at the age of eleven. At the age of fourteen he married a girl named Manekbai. A son and daughter were born to them.

Narsi led a peaceful life in Junagadh, till his wife's death in 1451 A.D. He also lost his children: his son first and his daughter, a few years later.

Narsi Mehta took his bereavements philosophically: "By His grace they have passed away. I feel no sorrow. We all have to leave this mortal frame one day. I can now pursue my devotion to Gopal without interruption", he said.

He danced and sang devotional songs composed by him day and night.

At the age of 53 Narsi left Junagadh and went to live in Mangrol, where he died at the age of 66 years.

The element of Bhakti or devotion, which is primarily a doctrine of adoration of a personalised God (*Ishtadevata*) which is predominant in Narsi Mehta's songs, is reminiscent of the same emotion in the *pāsurams* of the South Indian Alwars and the *tevarams* of the Nayanmars, who lived between 300 A.D. and 800 A.D.

Presumably, the Bhakti cult, born in South India, spread first in Karnataka and then to Maharashtra and culminated in Gujarat. Narsi Mehta's songs are the swansongs of this movement, which was lifegiving and lifesupporting at a time of foreign invasions of India.

CHANDIDAS

CHANDIDAS (1417-1477 A.D.)

Chandidas is one of the greatest Vaishnava poets of Bengal whose songs reverberate with religious fervour, literary grace and passionate love.

Sri Chaitanya who appeared on the scene after Chandidas used to listen to his songs and relish them.

The songs of Chandidas, extolling the love of Krishna and Radha in erotic imagery, are similar to the songs of Jayadeva, the Orissan saint and Vidyapati, the poet-saint of Mithila, Bihar.

Biographical details about Chandidas's life are scanty. He was probably born in a village named Chhatna near Bankura in Bengal. He was a high caste Brahmin village priest who fell in love with a low caste washerwoman named Rami, who appeared to him as Radha and inspired him to compose immortal songs depicting the love of Radha and Krishna.

Chandidas is the pioneer of the *Sahaja* movement of Bhakti in Bengal. In this spiritual approach, the body is sacred, and the pleasure of the senses is merged with the quest of the spirit. The Sahaja faith considered sublimation of erotic love as the easiest means of self-realisation. "The essence of beauty springs from the eternal play of man as Krishna and woman as Radha. Devoted lovers in the act of loving seek to reach the goal."

Chandidas and Rami have been compared to Dante and Beatrice. The spiritual approach of Chandidas, controversial as it may seem, is not an isolated one; it is in tune with that of many other Mystics of India, many of whom have adopted bridal mysticism in seeking union with God.

ANNAMACHARYA

ANNAMACHARYA (1424-1503 A.D.)

Annamacharya, one of the greatest Telugu poets and a great devotee of Sri Venkateswara of Tirupati, was born in 1424 A.D. in Tallapaka, a village in Cuddapah district of Andhra Pradesh, India. He lived upto the ripe old age of 79 years, dying in 1503 A.D.

The Deity in Tirupati was Annamacharya's obsession from a young age. He ran to Tirupati from his village and the first *darsan* of the Lord of Tirupati was an ecstatic experience for him and made him burst into devotional songs in praise of his chosen Deity.

Most of Annamacharya's songs centre round Lord Venkateswara of Tirupati. To him the Lord was most accessible.

He prays to Him, praises Him, talks with Him, argues with Him, quarrels with Him, pleads for His grace and surrenders to Him.

Annamacharya's *samkirtanas* or songs of praise of the Lord had a profound influence on Purandharadasa, who was a contemporary of Annamacharya and met him at Tirupati.

His influence is also seen in the works of the seventeenth century Telugu poet, Kshetrajna.

Devotional fervour is the main element in Annamacharya's compositions.

Like a true mystic, he came face to face with God and had a direct, immediate, firsthand, intuitive understanding of the Supreme Power, whose patent manifestation was Lord Venkateswara of Tirupati.

KABIR

KABIR (1440-1518 A.D.)

Kabir, the weaver-poet-saint of Uttar Pradesh, probably lived in the fifteenth century. Scholars differ about his exact dates of birth and death.

A Muslim by birth, he found Rama in Rahim and propounded a humanistic philosophy, cutting through the conventions of caste, creed and cult.

He mostly wrote in two-line couplets, known as *dohas,* expressing his intimate love for the Almighty.

Kabir was essentially a mystic. He had no teacher. His spiritual insights and philosophical thoughts were intuitive.

Kabir's poems are contained in the *Adi Granth,* the holy scripture of the Sikhs.

The mystic songs of Kabir, preaching the omnipresence of God and expressing a heartfelt desire for union with Him, are a precious legacy of not only India but all the world.

SANKARADEVA

SANKARADEVA (1449-1569 A.D.)

Sankaradeva, the Assamese Vaishnavite saint-reformer, was a passionate advocate of desireless devotion.

He preached equality of man before God.

"Treat all beings as God, and do not have caste distinctions" was his constant exhortation.

Sankaradeva was a many-sided personality. He was saint, religious teacher, singer, actor, social reformer and poet. He may be deemed the Assamese Tulsidas.

Sankaradeva was born in August-September 1449 as a Kayastha (non-Brahmin) boy in a village named Bardowa on the Brahmaputra river.

He married at the age of 21. He got a daughter at the age of 25, but his wife died soon after.

In 1481, at the age of 32, Sankaradeva went on a pilgrimage to holy places like Puri, Gaya, Mathura, Kurukshetra, etc.

He returned to Assam after 12 years in 1493 A.D. His pilgrimage had infused a new faith of love in him and he started preaching unswerving devotion to one God, Vishnu, who was also Krishna, *Ekasarana nāma Dharma.*

Sankaradeva composed devotional songs addressed to Lord Krishna, called *Bargits* (great songs).

Though he composed over 240 Bargits, only 34 remain. Rest were destroyed by fire.

Establishment of *Nāmghars* or village prayer houses was a unique innovation of Sankaradeva. His activities created a renaissance in Assam.

He died in 1569 A.D.

Sankaradeva was basically a religious mystic and his Vedantic Vaishnavism brought a message of love to the common people.

GURU NANAK

GURU NANAK (1469-1538 A.D.)

It is difficult to distinguish Guru Nanak from the other mystic saints of India like Kabir, Ravidas, Tukaram and others. The same passionate devotion and love of God pervades his songs which sing of the glory of God, "who is the Supreme Truth, Omnipresent, Unborn, Eternal".

Like most mystics, Guru Nanak was against excessive ritualism and abhorrent caste divisions, and did not advocate renunciation as a *sine qua non* for the attainment of spiritual bliss. The righteous way of life, according to Nanak, comprises: chanting the Holy Name of God, honest work, charity, keeping the body clean through proper ablutions, community service and prayer.

Nanak was born in 1469 at *Talwandi*, a village in Punjab. From early childhood he became interested in spiritual matters and by cultivating the company of wandering mendicants developed mastery over *Sādhu-bhāshā*, the language of the Sādhus, a variant of the Punjabi language in which he composed most of his songs.

Though he married and got two sons, Nanak left home and wandered for nearly forty years throughout the length and breadth of India awakening people to their inner self, which had its origin in the Universal Self, and challenging superstition and caste consciousness.

Ultimately he settled down with his family at a place known as *Kartarpur* on the banks of the river Ravi. He died in 1538 A.D.

Mysticism, Truth and simplicity combined with humility and God-intoxication invest the songs of Guru Nanak with an abiding appeal.

VALLABHACHARYA

VALLABHACHARYA (1479-1532 A.D.)

Vallabhacharya, the Vaishnavite saint, who propounded *Pushtimarga* or the path of Divine grace, was born at Champaranya (a village near Raipur) in 1479 A.D.

He was a contemporary of Sri Chaitanya, the Vaishnava saint of Bengal and the two met with each other a number of times. For both, Krishna was the total incarnation of God and love and devotion to their chosen Deity was the means to liberation.

While Chaitanya was excessively emotional in his approach to God, Vallabha was more intellectual, though there was no question about the depth and profundity of his devotion.

While Sri Chaitanya gave up family life early, Vallabha lived the life of a householder till the end.

Pushtimarga, preached by Vallabha, is a facet of his philosophical system known as *Suddha advaita* or pure Monism. According to Vallabha, individual souls are parts of God, like sparks from a blazing fire.

Vallabha's path of love and surrender to God to attain His Grace conforms to what Krishna said in the *Bhagavat Gita*: "Those who are wholly devoted to me, worship me, surrender all actions to me and meditate on me with undivided attention are speedily saved from the ocean of birth and death."

Vallabhacharya coined a beautiful term "*Brahma-sambandha*" which means *connecting with God* and laid great emphasis on it. He considered worship of God's images as useful aid in this "connecting with God". The image of Sri Nathji at the Nathdwara temple, near Udaipur is sacred to the followers of Vallabhacharya, as it is believed to have first materialised before him.

GURU AMAR DAS

GURU AMAR DAS (1479-1574 A.D.)

Guru Amar Das was the third Sikh Guru, succeeding Guru Angad. He was born in 1479 in Vasakha village in Punjab. A devout Vaishnavite in his earlier years, Guru Amar Das believed and taught that salvation could not result from observing external rituals but only by meditating on and chanting God's name.

Guru Amar Das compiled a two-volume collection of hymns, called *Mohan Pothi,* containing his own hymns along with those of Guru Nanak, Guru Angad and the mystics: Kabir, Namdev, Trilochan, Ram Prasad Sen, Ravidas and Jayadeva. This served as a nucleus for Guru Arjan Dev's compilation of the *Adi Granth,* the sacred book of the Sikhs.

Amar Das became a Guru at the ripe old age of 73 years. As Guru, he introduced several good customs like gathering to worship God on the first days of months like Vaisakhi, Magha and on Diwali, definitive rituals for birth and death, and eating together in disregard of caste distinctions. Guru Amar Das stressed the need for clean living and service of the people. He decried evil practices like *Sati* (widow's burning on funeral pyre).

Guru Amar Das died at the ripe old age of 95 years.

Finding his sons unfit to succeed him, he nominated his son-in-law Ram Das as his successor.

Guru Amar Das composed in all 907 hymns, of which 869 are in the Granth Sahib.

"Meditate on God's name and through the name, enter the state of supreme bliss" is the central theme of Guru Amar Das's songs.

ARUNAGIRINATHAR

ARUNAGIRINATHAR (15th Century A.D.)

Biographical details about Arunagirinathar are scanty. He is believed to have been born in Tiruvannamalai, the famous pilgrim centre, in which is located the Siva Temple known for its *Jyotirlinga.*

Arunagirinathar was a profligate in his youth, who suddenly transformed himself into a realised soul and became a devotee of Lord Subramanya (or Kumara, as he is known in North India).

Hymns of devotion burst forth from him and he composed over 16000 hymns, of which only 1307 are available today. These hymns are known as *Tiruppugazh,* which means in Tamil Holy Praise of God.

Arunagirinathar has written a few other small works as well like *Kandaranubhoothi, Kandarandadi, Kantharalankaram, Tiruvarutpa,* etc.

Most of his hymns were composed extempore during his visit to the various temples of Lord Subramanya in India and Sri Lanka.

Arunagirinathar sang his hymns in Tamil, but he mixed his Tamil expression with a liberal use of Sanskrit and poured forth melodious music, outstanding for its rhythmic patterns.

Arunagirinathar was a saint, a yogi, a poet and a great musical composer, apart from being a mystic who felt the presence of his beloved Deity Subramanya everywhere. The soul-stirring songs of this saint-singer have electrified subsequent generations and are sung with devotion in musical concerts even today.

SURDAS

SURDAS (1483-1563 A.D.)

The blind bard, Surdas was a contemporary of Akbar. He spent most of his time singing of his beloved Krishna, somewhere between Agra and Mathura. A meeting with Saint Vallabhacharya is said to have sparked poetry about the boyhood exploits of Sri Krishna.

The main works of Surdas are: *Sursagar, Sur Saravali* and *Sahityalahari.*

Surdas's songs overflow with pure, heartrending devotion.

But unlike Jayadeva and Vidyapati who deified Krishna, the Lover Surdas sang of child Krishna and his pranks. No Hindi poet has equalled Surdas in his knowledge of child psychology.

In his songs, Surdas shows his deep knowledge and understanding of the *Puranas,* especially the *Bhagavata.*

To hear Surdas's songs is to transport oneself to a spiritual world brimming with love, faith and devotion.

PURANDHARADASA

PURANDHARADASA (1484-1564 A.D.)

Purandharadasa, the Kannada saint-musician, was actually a Maratha by birth. He was born in a village near Pune in 1484, the son of a banker.

As a boy, he learnt music and Sanskrit; growing up was married to Saraswatibai, got involved in making money.

Suddenly one day, due to a miracle, the young banker renounced everything and left for Pandharpur and got initiated into asceticism. He travelled to various temples and pilgrim centres all over India and composed devotional songs numbering thousands.

Purandharadasa is considered the Grandfather of Carnatic music. About 8000 of his musical compositions survive today. Purandharadasa's songs extol the mercy of God and are immersed in intense devotion, though replete with references to myths and legends of Sri Krishna.

Having lived a full life of prolific creativity, Purandharadasa died in 1564 at the age of eighty.

Purandharadasa illustrated through his life Tyagaraja's dictum that music and devotion combined make the best path to God-realisation.

CHAITANYA MAHAPRABHU

CHAITANYA MAHAPRABHU (1486-1534 A.D.)

Chaitanya, the pioneer of the *Bhakti* movement in Bengal, was born on 18 February 1486 in Bengal. He became an ascetic at the age of 24 and travelled all over India from Bengal to Varanasi, South India, Dwaraka and Mathura returning to Nilachal near Puri in Orissa after 6 years.

Chaitanya advocated *Bhakti* or a pure love for Lord Krishna, which he considered superior to knowledge, meditation, yoga and charity.

He was strongly against the social inequities of the caste system and admitted men and women of all castes and religions into his extensive countrywide theistic movement.

For Chaitanya devotion to Krishna was the ultimate in spiritual aspiration, not even the liberation or the union with the Supreme which the advaitins like Sankara propagated. It was Chaitanya who established Brindavan near Mathura.

The songs of Chaitanya are steeped in this god-intoxicated love for and devotion to Sree Krishna.

Chaitanya's teaching was that the pure emotion of love is such a powerful force that it could transform human beings for the better and lead them on the path to ultimate bliss.

As in the case of many other saints, Chaitanya's family life went awry. His original name was Nemai Misra. His first wife was Lakshmi. She died, unable to bear the separation caused by her husband's long travels in the company of his fellow Vaishnavites.

He was forced to marry a second time a girl called *Vishnupriya* but Chaitanya had gone far into spiritual mysticism and god-intoxication that he could not be a good husband to Vishnupriya.

Chaitanya died at the age of fortyeight years.

The Vaishnavite followers of Chaitanya deem Radha and Krishna as one entity, assuming two different forms for the sake of the devotees. They hence worship Krishna as Radha.

The songs of Chaitanya fully bear out Chaitanya's philosophy of devotion, which to him was both the means and the end.

MEERA

MEERA (1498-1547 A.D.)

Meera, the princess-poet, saint-singer, was born in 1498 in a royal family of Mewar, Rajasthan.

From childhood, she became a devotee of Krishna.

She was married to Bhojaraja, a son of Rana Sanga who died while quite young.

Early widowhood helped Meera in her God-oriented ascetic life of prayer and devotion.

Like Andal of the seventh century, Meera saw herself as the bride of the Lord (Krishna) and poured forth her spiritual yearnings in soulful poetry.

Persecuted by her husband's brother, Meera had to leave Chittor and go to Brindavan. Her last few years were spent in Dwaraka, Gujarat. She died in 1547 A.D.

The God-intoxicated songs of Meera have transcended regional barriers and are sung all over India.

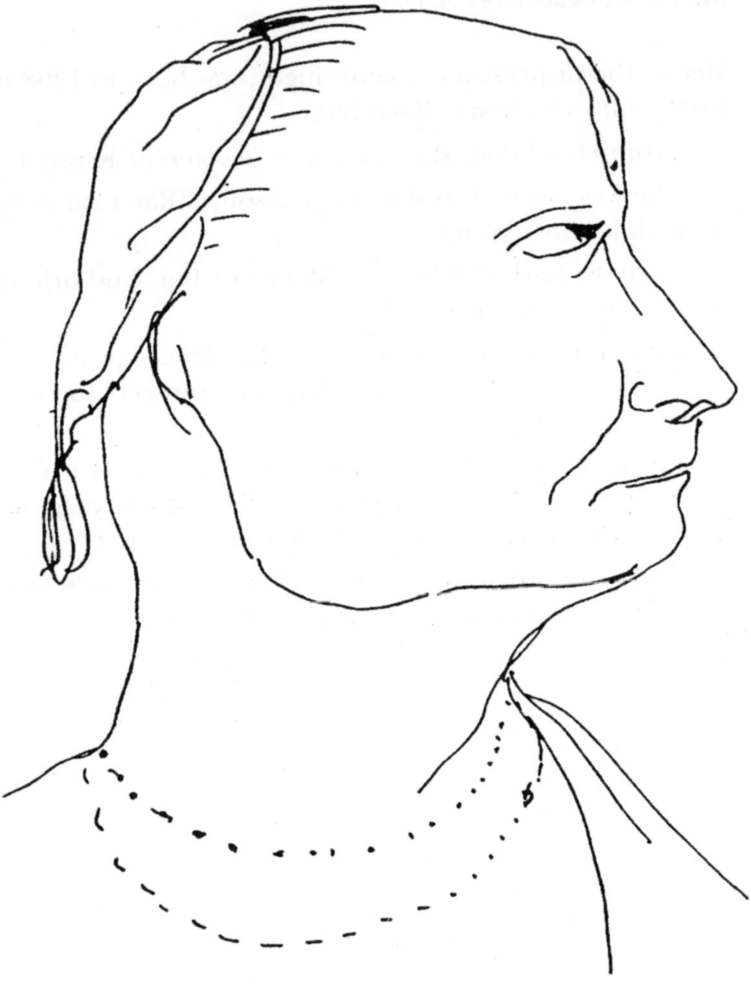

TULSIDAS

TULSIDAS (1532-1623 A.D.)

Details about Tulsidas's life are scanty.

He was probably born in 1532 at Rajapur in Uttar Pradesh and lived most of his life—alone and unapproachable—at Varanasi, where he died in 1623.

He was a contemporary of Akbar and Rana Pratap Singh of Udaipur.

Tulsidas's most famous work is the *Ramacharitamānas*, which deals with the story of Rama, Prince of Ayodhya, in loving devotion.

Tulsidas was an ardent devotee of Sri Rama as a divine incarnation of God. "The whole universe is full of Mother Sita and Lord Rama. With folded hands, I bow before them", he used to pray.

His other works include: *Krishna Gītāvali, Vinay Patrikā, Gītāvali, Kavitāvali, Dohāvali* etc. In all these works, Tulsi's devotion to God is explicit.

Tulsidas wrote his poetry in *Lok Bhasha* and *Braj Bhasha*, two dialects of Hindi.

RASKHAN

RASKHAN (1533-1588 A.D.)

Raskhan was born a Muslim, in Pihani, a village in the Hardoi district of Uttar Pradesh, India.

His original name was Saiyad Ibrahim.

Biographical details are scanty as to how, when and why Raskhan became a Vaishnavite devotee, madly intoxicated with love for God as Krishna and seeking ecstasy in visualising the amorous sports of the eternal Lover with the cowherdesses of Brindavan.

In his mystical devotion, Raskhan is in the line of poet-saints like Vidyapati and Jayadeva. Comparison with Kabir is limited to the fact that both were Muslim mystics. Kabir was a philosopher and social reformer, besides being a mystic poet.

Raskhan was solely immersed in unalloyed *Bhakti* or devotion to Krishna, the Lover. Nothing else mattered to him.

Raskhan's songs revel in descriptions of Krishnaleela, the amorous sports of youthful Krishna.

To Raskhan, as to Chaitanya, devotion to God was the means and the end.

While the sheer ecstasy of love permeates the poetry of Raskhan, the several allusions to mythological legends one finds in Raskhan's songs indicate his extensive knowledge of Puranic stories.

Raskhan is believed to have composed over 2000 verses, but only just over 600 have survived.

Raskhan figures among the 252 Vaishnavite saints eulogized in the work *Vaishnavon-ki-varta.*

EKNATH

EKNATH (1533-1606 A.D.)

Eknath, the householder saint of Maharashtra, was a poet and lover of God, who achieved renunciation while leading a life of a methodical and self-disciplined householder.

He was probably born in 1533 A.D. in Paithana, Maharashtra. He lost his parents early and was brought up by his grandparents. By the age of 12, Eknath had completed reading of Bhagavata.

Looking for a spiritual teacher to guide him, he went to Devagad, where a saint named Janardhana Swami took him as a disciple. Eknath worshipped his teacher as God and served him well.

Eknath mentions himself as the disciple of Janardhana in every song of his, in gratitude for his spiritual guidance.

Eknath visited all the sacred shrines and rivers in India, ultimately returning to his hometown Paithana.

As per his Guru's desire, Eknath married Girijabai and lived in Paithana till his death in 1606 A.D., conducting musical discourses and singing the praise of God.

The songs of Eknath, apart from being exquisite poetical pieces in Marathi language, are soaked in his devotion to God and reveal his altruism and innate humility.

Bhakti and *Jnana*, devotion and knowledge, mingled effortlessly in Eknath's life. Eknath advised constant chanting of God's name as a means of remembering Him continuously.

"Through love, the devotees can even become God. God and His devotees are akin to the Ocean and its waves" Eknath used to exhort. The culmination of *Bhakti* is union with God. "O! Lord! I am the singer, the hearer and the song" sang Eknath.

GURU RAMDAS

GURU RAMDAS (1534-1581 A.D.)

Guru Ramdas is the fourth Sikh Guru, among the ten Gurus of Sikhism.

The ten Gurus are: *Guru Nanak*, the founder of Sikhism, *Guru Angad*, Nanak's disciple, *Guru Amardas*, Angad's disciple, *Guru Ramdas*, Amardas's son-in-law, *Guru Arjan Dev*, Ramdas's son, *Guru Hargobind*, Arjan Dev's son, *Guru Har Rai*, Hargobind's grandson, *Guru Hari Krishen*, Har Rai's son, *Guru Tegh Bahadur*, Hargobind's son and *Guru Gobind Singh*, Tegh Bahadur's son.

Credit goes to Guru Ramdas for having got a large tank dug, around which the city of Amritsar was built by his son Arjan Dev.

All the Sikh Gurus were profoundly influenced by the exponents of the Bhakti movement, and all their songs emphasize the chanting of the Lord's name as a means to liberation. Guru Ramdas is no exception.

The preaching of Guru Nanak pervades the songs of Guru Ramdas:

"There is One God. His entity is the Truth. He is the Creator. He is without fear. He is without enmity. Of timeless form, He never dies or takes birth. He is self-effulgent. He can be realised only through His grace."

This is not different from the Hindu concept of Godhead.

Another remarkable fact to be noted is that Guru Ramdas, like all the other Sikh Gurus, refers to God as *Hari, Rama, Govind, Madhusudan, Murari, Narahari,* etc. all of them Vaishnavite epithets applied to God.

DADU DAYAL

DADU DAYAL (1544-1603 A.D.)

Dadu Dayal, the mystic poet-saint of Rajasthan, was born in 1544 A.D. in Ahmedabad, Gujarat in a Muslim family. He was a cotton cleaner by profession.

Dadu Dayal, like Kabir who lived a few years earlier to him, sang of the omnipresence of God and expressing a heartfelt desire for union with Him. He was an *advaitin*, deeming the phenomenal world illusory or *Māyā*.

He was a mystic seeking direct communion with God, in an attitude of bridal mysticism (like Andal, Meera and the Alwars).

He was *Vaishnavite* in holding that chanting the name of God, Rama, was a means of God-realisation.

Dadu's compassionate nature won him the surname *Dayāl* (lit. the kind one).

Emperor Akbar appears to have met Dadu and was deeply impressed by his spirituality.

Dadu frequently used the images of river, ocean, shore, flood, pot, etc. to describe the human condition and worldly existence and how only God the navigator could provide liberation from the cycle of birth and death.

Dadu Dayal was against religious bigotry and the religious barriers that divided men.

God was within everyone and the way to realise Him was through devotion and constant remembrance by chanting His name.

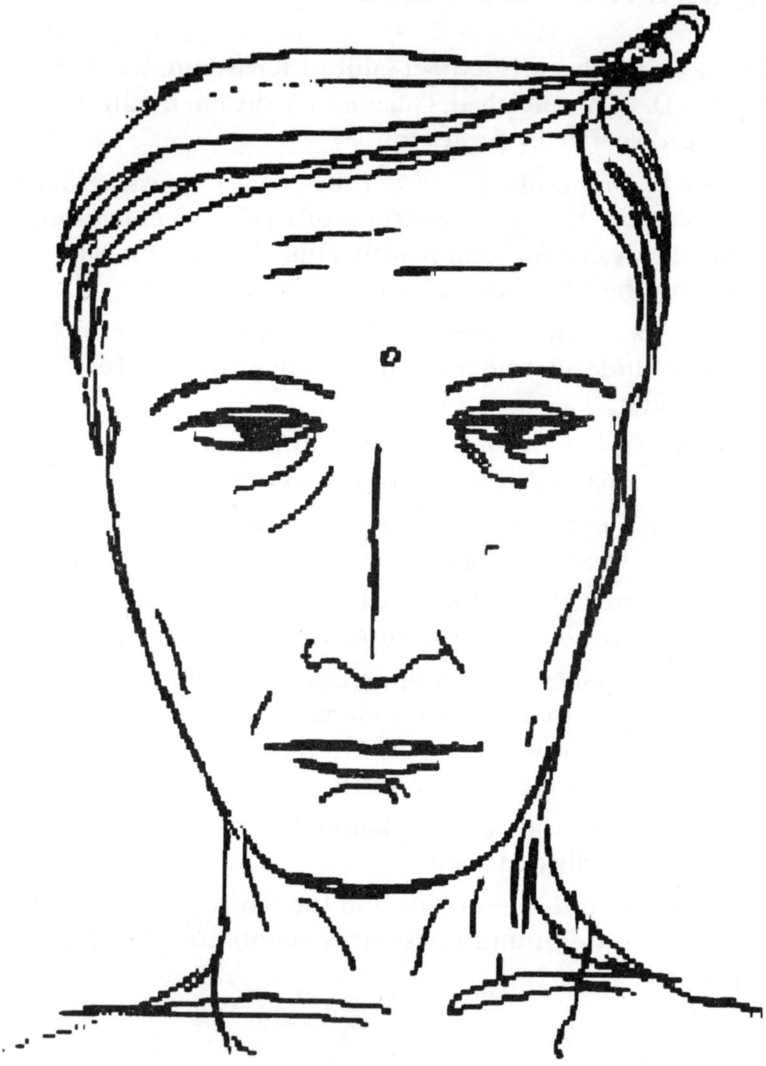

POONTANAM

POONTANAM (1547-1640 A.D.)

Poontanam is one of the foremost mystic poet-saints of Kerala. A poor Nambudiri Brahmin, who lacked any erudite scholarship, he was a great devotee of God and poured forth his love, devotion and faith in a poetical language, easily understood by the common people.

A contemporary of the more scholarly and erudite *Narayana Bhattadiri*, who composed the famous *Narayaneeyam* in praise of Krishna, the Deity in the famous temple of Guruvaayoor, Poontanam was fascinated by the mythical exploits of child Krishna and sang of them in short hymns which are sung even today in many Kerala homes at dusk.

A personal tragedy—the accidental death of his son—made Poontanam deeply philosophical and he composed the famous *Jnānapāna*, which deals with the transience of life and the need to seek peace by chanting the holy name of God.

His other work the *Bhāshakarnamritam* deals with the glory of Child-God Krishna.

Poontanam, Narayana Bhattadiri and Ezhuttacchan may be deemed the Trinity of saint-poets of Kerala.

Narayana Bhattadiri is famous for his magnum opus *Narayaneeyam*, composed in Sanskrit, while Ezhuttacchan is known for his work *Harināmakirtanam.*

Poontanam sang in very simple Malayalam, but his profound devotion to God elevates his work to a high level.

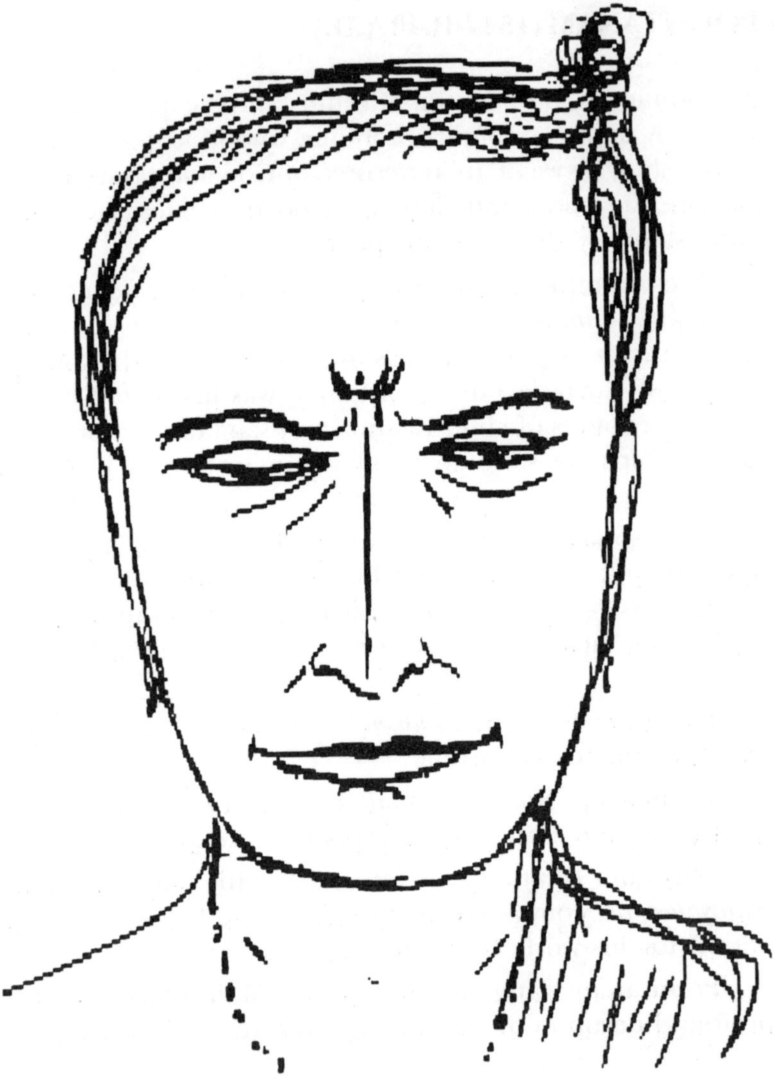

NARAYANA BHATTADIRI

MEPPATTOOR NARAYANA BHATTADIRI (1560-1655 A.D.)

Meppattoor Narayana Bhattadiri, the author of the famous devotional work *Narayaneeyam*, was a Nambudiri Brahmin of Kerala and one of the greatest mystic saint-poets of India. Meppattoor was the name of his family, located in the Ponnani Taluq of Kerala.

Struck with paralysis, he sought refuge at the feet of the Deity in the *Guruvaayoor* temple, Sri Krishna and composed his magnum opus *Narayaneeyam*, comprising 1036 verses in Sanskrit dealing with the various incarnations of the Lord, beginning with the one as fish. He completed the work in 100 days and on the hundredth day, he was totally cured of his malady.

Though the spirit of devotion pervades and predominates in the songs of Narayana Bhattadiri, his leaning towards Advaita (the philosophical doctrine propounded by Sankara about the identity of the individual soul with the Supreme Spirit) is unmistakable.

Bhakti or devotion is only a means to the attainment of liberation or union with God.

Surrender, with the devotion at the feet of God, leads to His grace, which is a prerequisite for the knowledge of self-realisation.

The beauty of the Sanskrit language, the intense devotion of Bhattadiri and his profound philosophic approach invest his songs with the aura of immortality.

GURU ARJAN DEV

GURU ARJAN DEV (1563-1606 A.D.)

Guru Arjan Dev, the fifth Sikh Guru and the youngest son of Guru Ram Das, the fourth Guru, whom he succeeded, was a mystical poet, who composed 2216 hymns, proclaiming the glory of God, the need for constant devotion to God and the efficacy of chanting His name.

Though Guru Ram Das built a brick temple at Amritsar, it was Arjan Dev who extended it and built the Golden Temple there.

To Guru Arjan Dev goes the credit of compiling the *Adi Granth* or the *Granth Sahib*, the Holy book of the Sikhs, which is an anthology of hymns of various saints, earlier Gurus and Arjan Dev's own 2216 hymns.

Guru Arjan Dev completed the compilation of Adi Granth in 1604. In 1606, he was executed by the intolerant Emperor Jahangir and became the first Sikh martyr.

Guru Arjan Dev's magnum opus is *Sukhmani.*

A perusal of Guru Arjan Dev's compositions reveals the patent fact that the names used by him (as by all Sikh Gurus) to refer to God are the Hindu epithets like *Hari, Rama, Govind, Gopal,* etc.

Viewed in this light, the Sikh Gurus are not very different from the other Hindu mystic poet-saints of India.

TUNCHATTU EZHUTTACCHAN

TUNCHATTU EZHUTTACCHAN (16th Century A.D.)

Tunchattu Ezhuttacchan, the great poet and spiritual savant from Kerala, is one of the Greats in Malayalam Literature.

Ezhuttacchan, Poontanam and Meppattoor Narayana Bhattadiri, who were believed to have been contemporaries, form the Trinity of poet saints from Kerala.

The *Harinamasamkeertanam* of Ezhuttacchan, *Jnaanapaana* of Poontanam and *Narayaneeyam* of Narayana Bhattadiri form the spiritual landmarks of Kerala.

While Narayana Bhattadiri wrote his *Narayaneeyam* in Sanskrit, Ezhuttacchan and Poontanam wrote their works in Malayalam.

Biographical details about Ezhuttacchan are scanty. He was born (probably in early 16th century) in a village 25 miles south of Kozhikode, North Kerala.

While he spent most of his life in his home village, he moved in old age to a village near Chittoor, near Palghat, where he established a *mutt* and continued his spiritual pursuits.

Though *Harinamasamkeertanam* conveys his philosophical ideas soaked in the teachings of Vedanta, Ezhuttacchan's fame rests on his monumental work, *Adhyatma Ramayana.* This work compels comparison with the works of Kamban and Tulsidas.

But *Harinamasamkeertanam* of Ezhuttacchan is a wonderful work combining *Bhakti* and *Jnāna*, devotion and knowledge. In simple language, understandable by common people, its verses convey the essence of the Upanishads.

KANAKADASA

KANAKADASA (16th Century A.D.)

Kanakadasa, who was a contemporary of Purandharadasa, was a shepherd by birth. He was a disciple of Vyasaraya, who was probably Purandharadasa's teacher as well.

Kanakadasa was born in a village named Bada in Dharwar district of Karnataka. His parents died when he was very young and as an orphan was brought up by relatives.

Kanakadasa was devoted to Lord Krishna from childhood. There is a story connected with Kanakadasa and the Udupi temple.

Kanakadasa came to the Udupi temple but was denied admission, because of his low caste. He went to the rear of the temple and prayed. As a result of his prayers, the image in the temple turned towards the direction where Kanakadasa was standing and the temple wall collapsed enabling Kanakadasa to have *darsan* of the Deity.

Even today the opening is called *Kanaka's window* at the Udupi Temple.

The Ruler of Anegonde (a part of the Vijayanagar Empire) made Kanaka a chieftain in charge of Bankapur, where he lived and worshipped at the temple of Adi Keshava of Kaginele.

Kanakadasa lived for 98 years and travelled throughout the country singing praises of God.

The songs of Kanakadasa, though full of devotion, have also a philosophical content. Two of his songs fully bear this out: *Tanu ninnadu* and *Nee mayeyolago.*

Kanakadasa was a bitter critic of the caste system. He brings this out in his song: *Kula Kula vennu,* in which he asks: "*What is the caste of the Soul? What is the caste of Life? When God who resides in the inner soul blesses, what caste is a caste?*"

RAHIM

RAHIM (16th Century A.D.)

Rahim, whose full name was Nawab Abdur-Rahim Khan-i-Khanan, was a poet in Emperor Akbar's court.

He was a scholar well versed in Persian, Arabic, Turkish, Sanskrit, Braj Bhasha and Avadhi.

He was a contemporary of Tulsidas.

Rahim's obsession was the amorous sports of Lord Krishna with the Gopis.

Like Surdas, Rahim expresses, in a few couplets, the yearning of forlorn Gopis for union with Krishna and in others the bliss of meeting with Krishna.

The radiant beauty of *Srinathji* lured the Pathan Rahim and made him as lovelorn as the Gopis of Brindavan.

In one couplet, Rahim exclaims:

> "*The eyes are all too full of Mohan's beauty*
> *How can there be room for other beauties?*
> *Finding the caravansarai full, every new*
> *traveller turns away from the gates.*"

Passionate love, powerful imagery, an outstanding literary acumen and a deep knowledge of the myths and legends of India enabled Rahim to pour out in beautiful *Braj Bhasha* lyrics that elevate us to ecstatic heights of spiritual experience.

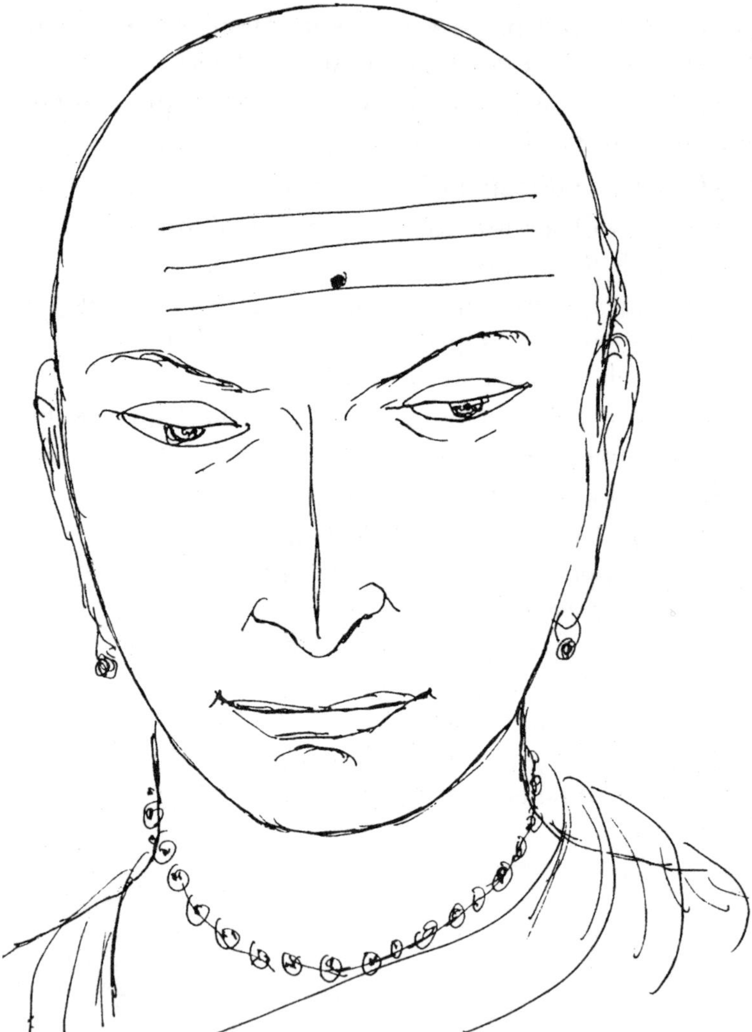

APPAYYA DIKSHITAR

APPAYYA DIKSHITAR (16th-17th Century A.D.)

Sri Appayya Dikshitar, the renowned scholar and mystic poet-philosopher of South India, probably lived in the 16th-17th century A.D.

He was born in the village of *Adayappalam*, near *Virinchipuram*, Kanchi, in a family of philosophical and devotional poets. Appayya, a born devotee of Lord Siva, considered *Bhakti* or devotion and the resultant grace of God as indispensable for ultimate liberation.

Like many other mystic saints, Appayya had misgivings about his own devotion to God and wanted to test the strength of his devotion. He hence drank the maddening juice of *Kanakaphala* and in a delirious state poured out fifty devotional songs, which were taken down by his disciples. These fifty verses constitute the famous *Ātmarpana Stuti* (lit. song of self-surrender).

These songs are soaked in the deepest devotion and seek God's help in crossing the abyss of the phenomenal world.

Appayya Dikshitar's famous prayer *Mārgabandhustotram*, in which the Lord is deemed the friend on the road, is usually recited on commencement of journeys for a safe and trouble-free arrival at the destination.

Appayya Dikshitar implies that the Lord's guidance is required not only for earthly journeys but also on the spiritual path to salvation.

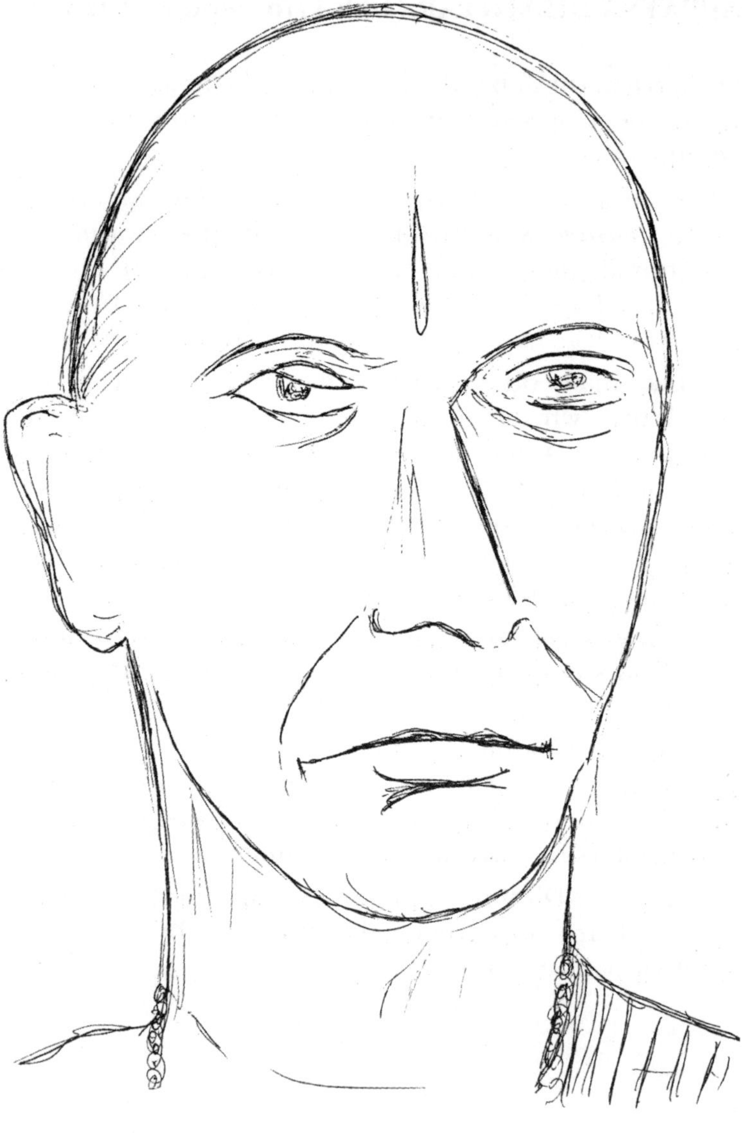

KSHETRAJNA

KSHETRAJNA (17th Century A.D.)

Kshetrajna, the most outstanding composer of musical texts in the Telugu language, lived in the first half of the 17th century.

His original name was *Varadayya,* but the name Kshetrajna was given to him because of his visits to the various temples of South India. *Kshetrajna* means knower of temples.

He was born in the village of Muvva in Krishna district of Andhra Pradesh. There is a temple in this village to Krishna as the cowherd, the Deity therein being called *Muvva Gopala* (the Divine Cowherd with Jingling Bells).

Kshetrajna, in an attitude of bridal mysticism and deeply felt love for his chosen Lord, glorifies the exploits of the Lord the Lover by portraying the all-absorbing passion of the Gopis for Gopala: joy of union, sorrow in separation, hope in waiting and despair in lover's betrayal.

The songs of Kshetrajna, ideally suited for music and dance, refer, in erotic imagery, to the various Deities in the temples of Kanchipuram, Chidambaram, Madurai, Srirangam, Tanjavur etc.

Treating God as the Lover is a tradition adopted by spiritual aspirants in India like the Alwars and Nayanmars (especially Nammalwar and Manikkavachakar) and the Vaishnavite saints like Chandidas, Vidyapati and Jayadeva.

The individual soul is the Gopi or Nayika seeking union with the Supreme Being who is the sought after Lover!

SADASIVA BRAHMENDRA

SADASIVA BRAHMENDRA (17th Century A.D.)

Sadasiva Brahmendra was one of the most eminent Telugu poet-philosopher-composers of the 17th century A.D. Sadasiva Brahmendra became a recluse from a young age and wandered from place to place totally naked and observing silence.

He is believed to have been made a sanyaasi by the 57th head of Kanchi Kamakoti Peetha.

He was a *jīvanmukta* (i.e. one who is liberated even while living). Though he was an *Advaitin,* he composed devotional songs in Sanskrit extolling the greatness of Deities like Krishna and Rama, the personal manifestations of the Divine (*Saguna Brahman*).

He, however, also composed songs on the *Nirguna Brahman* (the formless Supreme) propounding the advaitic philosophy that everything is a manifestation of God.

As Prof. V. Raghavan remarked: "*Sadasiva Brahmendra sang the symphony of Brahman.*"

The work of Sadasiva Brahmendra influenced greatly the compositions of Muttuswami Dikshitar and to a lesser extent those of Tyagaraja.

The term "*Paramahamsa*" (One who has renounced the world and has realised the Self) occurs in the songs of this advaitic saint as a mark of his authorship.

BHADRACHALA RAMADAS

BHADRACHALA RAMADAS (17th Century A.D.)

Bhadrachala Ramadas, the Telugu mystic saint-poet, lived during the period the Qutub Shahis (Muslim rulers) were ruling in Golconda.

Tani Shah (Abul Hassan) was the ruler, under whom Ramadas's uncle Madanna worked as Minister.

Ramadas's original name was *Gopanna.* He came to be called Ramadas or servant of Rama, because of his devotion to Rama.

Ramadas spent his time seeking the company of devotees of Rama and arranging dramatic enactment of Puranic stories and mass singing of devotional songs. His devotion to Rama was so intense that he saw Rama in all beings and everywhere. He became the Tahsildar (a revenue official) of Bhadrachalam taluq.

The Rama Temple in Bhadrachalam was in a damaged state and Ramadas, intent on renovating the temple and providing jewellery for the temple Deity, began diverting state revenues for the temple. He was promptly imprisoned for this misappropriation of funds.

He spent 12 years in jail and during this period poured out his devotion to Rama in heartrending songs.

The story goes that Rama and Lakshmana went to Tani Shah in person and remitted the entire amount due from Ramadas and Tani Shah overpowered by this spectacle went to Ramadas, released him and sent him with enough money to continue his service to Rama of Bhadrachala.

Ramadas's devotional songs, though rendered in the Telugu language, are embellished by the use of Sanskrit. They became popular all over the country.

Tyagaraja, a devotee of Rama, during a later period, admired and saluted Ramadas in a few songs.

Ramadas's songs are sung in Carnatic music recitals even today.

TUKARAM

TUKARAM (1608-1650 A.D.)

Saint Tukaram was born in a small village named Dehu in Maharashtra in the year 1608. Like his parents, he was a devotee of Vitthala of the temple at Pandharpur.

In his life, Tukaram underwent a lot of misery, including extreme poverty. His family business ran into losses, his first wife died and his second wife, Jijabai, proved to be a shrew. But Tukaram remained unflinching in his devotion to the Lord of Pandharpur and composed mellifluous songs to His Divine Master.

Tukaram's songs are known as *Abhangs* (meaning: unbreakable ones).

What he sang was dutifully recorded by two of his disciples Gangaram Maval and Santaji Teli and transferred to posterity. Today they are a part of the psyche of the people of Maharashtra.

Tukaram was a contemporary of Shivaji, who was one of his admirers.

Tukaram conducted prayer meetings, singing *bhajans*, to which a large number of people flocked and his fame spread.

He died in 1650.

As one of his disciples declared: No one could match Tukaram in *Jnāna*, *Bhakti* and *Vairāgya* (knowledge, devotion and detachment).

His songs display rustic simplicity, deep devotion and a frank intimacy with his beloved personal God *Vitthala of Pandharpur.*

SAMARTHA RAMADAS

SAMARTHA RAMADAS (1608-1681 A.D.)

Samartha Ramadas is one of the five major mystic saints of Maharashtra, the other four being Jnaneswar, Namdev, Tukaram and Eknath.

Samartha Ramadas was born in 1608 A.D., on the Ramanavami day. His childhood name was Narayan. He ran away from home at the age of eleven, and practised penance on the banks of Krishna river for twelve years. His chosen Deity was Sri Rama. From the age of 24 to 36, he travelled all over India. In the Himalayas, he visited Badrinath, Kedarnath and Kailasanath.

He became a monk and established his Ashram at Chabai on the banks of the Krishna river. His name "Samartha Ramadas" spread far and wide. The Maharashtra Ruler, Shivaji, became his disciple.

The story goes that when Ramadas extended his begging bowl, Shivaji put a gift deed of his entire kingdom into it. Ramadas returned it to him, saying: "Rule on my behalf. God bless you!"

Though he himself was a monk, Ramadas did not preach running away from the world to attain spiritual salvation. According to him one could be active in the material world and yet be spiritual.

In his magnum opus, *Dasabodha*, he expounds the philosophy of devotion or *Bhakti Yoga*. For *Bhakti* it is necessary to have a chosen Deity or *Ishtadevata*, like Rama in the case of Ramadas.

Ramadas was very fond of music and set his songs in various ragas. He even dealt with the nuances of music in some of his songs.

Samartha Ramadas died in 1681 A.D.

GURU TEGH BAHADUR

GURU TEGH BAHADUR (1621-1675 A.D.)

Guru Tegh Bahadur, the martyred ninth Guru of the Sikhs, wrote soul-stirring songs about the bliss of remembering, loving and adoring God.

For Guru Tegh Bahadur, the only true relationship in this ephemeral world was one with God.

He was born in 1621 A.D. at Amritsar, the youngest son of his parents. For 20 years, he spent a quiet, studious and contemplative life in Patna, where his son, the famous Guru Govind Singh, was born.

Tegh Bahadur became the ninth Sikh Guru in 1664 A.D.

He settled down at Anandpur, on the banks of Sutlej.

Guru Tegh Bahadur was living during the period of Aurangzeb, the fanatical tyrant.

There is a story that Tegh Bahadur told his son about Aurangzeb's tyranny and said: "Grave are the burdens which the earth carries. She will be redeemed only if a truly worthy person comes forward to sacrifice his head."

The precocious son, Govind said: "Father, who could be better than you for such a noble deed?"

Govind's words proved prophetic.

Guru Tegh Bahadur challenged Aurangzeb and was publicly executed on 11th November, 1675 A.D.

His martyrdom rejuvenated the fight against fundamentalist tyranny.

Tegh Bahadur's devotional songs have been popular, generation after generation, and are a great solace to people in suffering.

BULLEH SHAH

BULLEH SHAH (1680-1752 A.D.)

Bulleh Shah, the Sufi saint of Punjab, was a Vedantin, calm and serene, full of love, kindness and mercy.

God was his Beloved and he yearned for a vision of his Beloved.

In his devotional songs, called *kafis*, he sang

> *"Drink a cup of love and you forget all!*
> *God resides in each and every house.*
> *And he permeates every human soul.*
> *Our preceptor dwells within us.*
> *When I fell in love, I realized this."*

Bulleh Shah was born in 1680 A.D. in Lulani near Lahore.

Though he was a Chief of a town and had abundant wealth, he left it all to become a poor mendicant.

Once the Muslim priests asked him who he was. Bulleh Shah replied, like a true Vedantin: "I am He" (*Anal Hauq*).

At another time, Bulleh Shah declared himself to be the Emperor. His empire was that of the Self, which was immortal, infinite and limitless.

Bulleh Shah lived a life of total renunciation and unflinching devotion to God.

He died at the age of 72 in 1752 A.D.

A disciple of the Sufi saint, Mian Mir, Bulleh Shah realized the hollowness and transience of worldly possessions.

Swami Sivananda remarked: "Bulleh Shah's songs contain the fundamentals of Advaita Vedanta."

SHAHJI MAHARAJA

SHAHJI MAHARAJA (1684-1710 A.D.)

Shahji Maharaja, son of Ekoji Raja, the short-lived King of Tanjore—he lived for hardly 26 years—was an intense devotee of the Deity in the temple of Tiruvarur, known as Tyagaraja.

He was a great patron of literature and arts. He was a masterly scholar in Sanskrit, apart from being proficient in other languages like Telugu, Marathi and Hindustani.

Shahji's scholarship in Sanskrit and his knowledge of music, combined with his devotion to God enabled him to compose moving songs set to mellifluous music. All his songs are in Sanskrit.

Shahji Maharaja began the tradition of *nādopāsanā* or practice of music with devotion as a means of God realisation, subsequently proved effective by the Trinity of Carnatic music: Tyagaraja, Syama Sastri and Muttuswami Dikshitar.

Shahji Maharaja's treatise on *rāgas* or musical melodies, written in Telugu, is in the famous Saraswati Mahal Library in Tanjavur (Tanjore).

Apart from the various hymns to Lord Tyagaraja of Tiruvarur, Shahji composed a beautiful opera on the Deity in Telugu entitled *"Pallavi Seva Prabandham"* which is enacted daily in the temple service.

The early death of this mystic devotee is an example of the dictum: "Those whom God loves die Young."

NARAYANA TEERTHA

NARAYANA TEERTHA (18th Century A.D.)

Narayana Teertha was an Advaitic saint who cultivated music combined with devotion (*Nādopāsanā*) as a means of spiritual evolution.

In beautiful Sanskrit, he has composed musical songs describing the amorous sports of Sree Krishna.

His major work, *Krishna Leela Tarangini,* contains over 150 songs to be rendered in forty different ragas and are the ones popularly sung by leading Carnatic musicians in their concerts.

Narayana Teertha was born in Andhra Pradesh. He went on an extensive pilgrimage, which covered major pilgrim centres like Puri, Srikakulam, Sobhanagiri, Vedagiri and Varahur in Tanjavur district, Tamil Nadu.

He attained Samadhi at Tiruppunturuti (a place between Tanjavur and Tiruvaiyyar).

Narayana Teertha's adoration of Krishna is evident in every song of his. Rendered in mellifluous Sanskrit, his songs are music to the ears of devotees and transport them to an enchanting world of devotion and spirituality.

The songs of Narayana Teertha influenced Tyagaraja, the later savant who also poured out his devotion in soulful music.

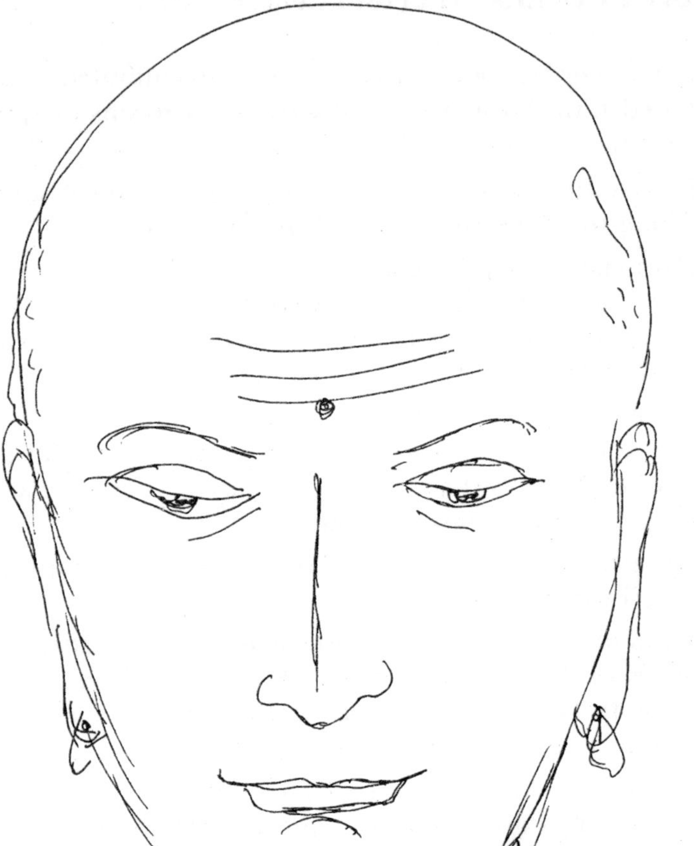

ABHIRAMI BHATTAR

ABHIRAMI BHATTAR (18th Century A.D.)

Abhirami Bhattar was a priest at the temple of Abhirami in Tirukkadayur on the banks of the river Kaveri. He is believed to have lived about 250-300 years ago.

His original name was Subramanian. His father's name: Amrita Linga Iyer. He was born in the *Kausika Gotra.* His family lineage was one of musical talent and devotion to the Deity at the Tirukkadayur temple: Goddess Abhirami.

Like Ramakrishna Paramahamsa, who was always God-intoxicated, worshipping at the Kali temple in Dakshineswar, Calcutta, Abhirami Bhattar, full of devotion to his Beloved goddess, appeared to be a man out of his mind to his contemporary peers.

During the period Abhirami Bhattar lived, the Maharashtra Ruler Sarabhoji Raja was ruling in Tanjore.

There is a legend that when the king visited the temple, on a new moon day, Bhattar in a fit of spiritual ecstasy declared that it was a full moon day.

The king was surprised, but that night, he had a dream that Goddess Abhirami threw one of her ear ornaments into the dark sky and created an illusion of the full moon.

Realising that the priest was an evolved soul, the ruler conferred the title of *Abhirami Bhattar* on him.

Abhirami Bhattar's fame rests on his work, *Abhirami Antadi* a poem of 100 verses, extolling the beauty of Goddess Abhirami, though he has composed a few other works.

This work indicates how a true devotee of God can pour out his love and devotion in mellifluous poetry.

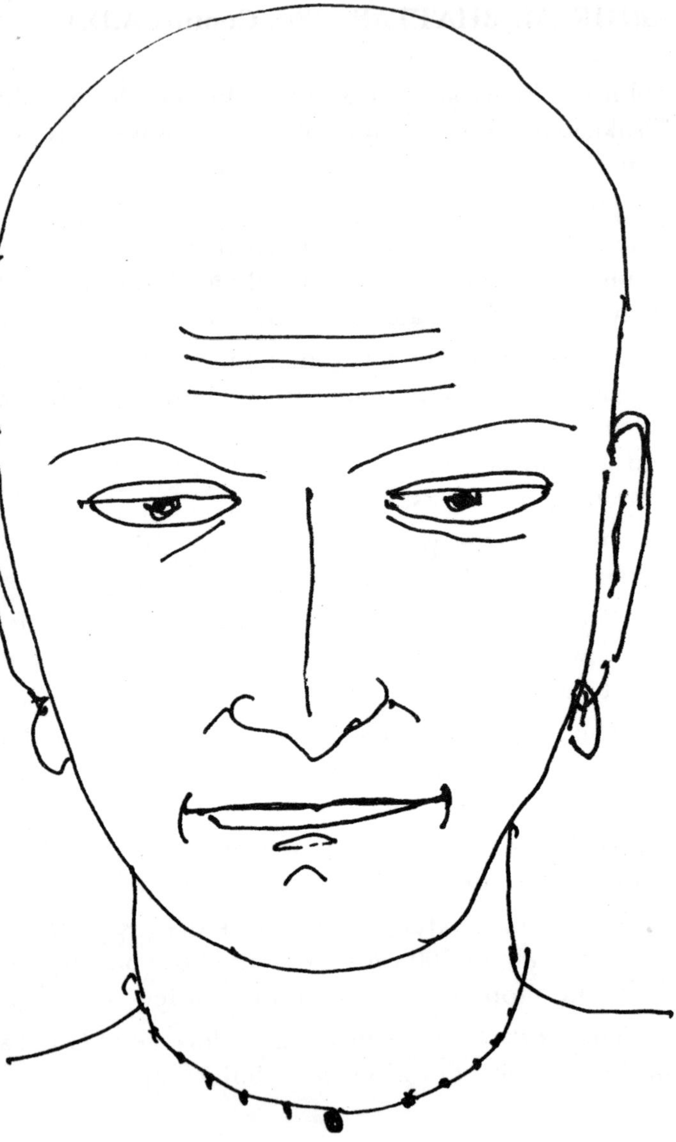

MUTTU TANDAVAR

MUTTU TANDAVAR (18th Century A.D.)

Particular temples of India have been sources of inspiration for several mystic poet-sages of India.

Chidambaram temple where Lord Nataraja is deemed to be ever dancing, inspired Gopalakrishna Bharati to compose his immortal work *Nandanar Charitam.*

Muttu Tandavar is another saint inspired by the Chidambaram temple to pour out devotional songs.

Biographical details about Muttu Tandavar are scanty.

He is believed to have lived in the 18th century.

Though born in *Sirkāzhi,* he used to walk a distance of 12 miles daily to worship at the Chidambaram temple.

Legend has it that by Divine Grace he was cured of a terrible disease and prompted to compose and sing devotional songs eulogizing the Deity in the Chidambaram temple.

Accordingly, Muttu Tandavar composed songs conveying his ecstatic experience of communion with the Lord and glorification of the beauty, grace and benefaction of the Cosmic Dancer.

Only 60 of his songs are available today. But each song is a veritable treasure of devotion, God-intoxication and musical melody.

According to a legend, Muttu Tandavar joined the Supreme Being, while singing one of his songs.

Muttu Tandavar's songs are an inseparable part of every Carnatic musician's repertoire.

OOTTUKKADU VENKATASUBBA IYER

OOTTUKKADU VENKATASUBBA IYER (1700-1765 A.D.)

Oottukkadu Venkatasubba Iyer was born in Mannargudi, a village in Tamilnad, around the beginning of the 18th century, the son of Ramachandra Vathoolar and Kamala Nayani Ammal. Though born in Mannargudi, he spent most of his time in the village of Oottukkadu. Hence the name Oottukkadu.

The young Venkatasubban wanted to learn music, but could not find a suitable Guru. His mother asked him to accept Lord Krishna himself as Guru.

He became a mystical devotee of Krishna, kept himself aloof from everyone and composed and sang his songs during the night so as not to be seen or heard by crowds.

He composed over 1000 songs in Tamil and Sanskrit.

When he sang his songs he danced in ecstatic bliss.

Oottukkadu Venkatasubba Iyer was a lifelong celibate and bachelor.

Like Surdas, Oottukkadu Venkatasubba Iyer was fascinated by the childhood pranks of Lord Krishna.

The song *"Tāye Yasode"*, one of the most popular and widely sung songs of Oottukkadu, recalls to one's mind Surdas's *"Madhukar syām hamāre"* and Subramania Bharati's "*Teerada Vilayattu pillai*".

The songs of Oottukkadu Venkatasubba Iyer are one more example, in the long line of the mystic poets of India, as to how devotion to and love of the dark-hued image of Lord Krishna has inspired such elevating poetry, across the barriers of time and region and language.

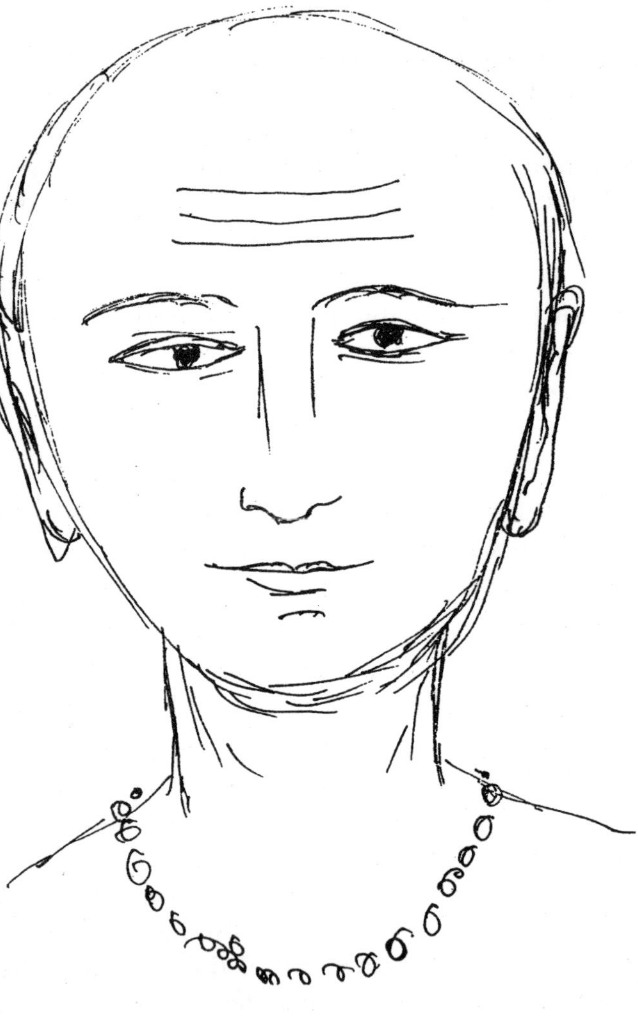

TAYUMANAVAR

TAYUMANAVAR (1705-1742 A.D.)

The songs of Tayumanavar, the Saivite saint of Tamil Nadu, are like those of the Kerala saint, Ezhuttacchan, soaked in devotion, combined with the spirit of Advaita.

Tayumanavar was born in 1705 A.D., the son of Ketilya Pillai, who lived in the town of Vedaranyam and worked as the Estate Manager for the Raja of Tiruchirapalli.

He was named Tayumanavar after the name of the Deity in the temple in Tiruchirapalli, by whose grace his father believed he was born.

At a very early age, Tayumanavar learnt the Upanishads, Puranas etc. After his father's death, he became the estate manager, at the age of 14.

He was a seeker after Truth and told the pundits in the Raja's court to "*Find out the Truth*".

He became the disciple of a spiritual teacher called *Maunaguru.*

Though he married and got a son, after his wife's death, he became a *Sannyasin.* He left home with a loin cloth and spent his time practising Yoga and meditation.

He began to compose soulful devotional songs which were collected and published by his disciple, *Arulayar.*

Tayumanavar went to Ramanathapuram and died in 1742 A.D.

According to Swami Sivananda, "*Tayumanavar was an embodiment of the Vedas. His songs of realisation, sung by everybody throughout South India, contain elevating, soul-stirring, sublime thoughts and penetrate deep into the heart of hearers.*"

RAMPRASAD SEN

RAMPRASAD SEN (1723-1803 A.D.)

Ramprasad, the Bengali saint-poet, who was born of poor parents at Kumarhatti in Nadia district of Bengal, was a devotee of the Divine Mother.

Though he remained a householder, he surrendered himself totally to *Kāli.*

While working as a bookkeeper, his mind was so immersed in the Divine Mother that instead of entering figures, he wrote poems. His employer sent him home with a pension, so that he did not have to work for a living.

Ramprasad was a *Shāktā,* pouring out his devotion in intimate, simple, sweet songs addressed to the Mother, whom he considered a part of the family.

Ramprasad had a daughter who lovingly looked after him and Ramprasad often imagined that the Divine Mother herself came down as his daughter to do his chores.

Four hundred of Ramprasad's songs survive today. These are sung even today in every Bengali household. He composed a raga or melody known as *Rāmprasadi,* in which some of his songs are sung.

Ramprasad was against cruel practices like animal sacrifice and meaningless idolatory.

Like a true mystic, he believed in total surrender and complete communion with God as a panacea for the ills of the world. His songs reflect this approach of his and are full of God-intoxicated love and devotion.

SYAMA SASTRI

SYAMA SASTRI (1762-1827 A.D.)

Syama Sastri is the eldest of the Trinity of Carnatic music-saints, the other two being Muttuswami Dikshitar and Tyagaraja.

Syama Sastri was born at Tiruvarur, but went to Tanjavur at the age of nineteen and settled down there.

Syama Sastri was born in a family, members of which were worshippers of the Divine Mother for generations.

Devotion to Divine Mother was hence part of his bloodstream.

Even from an early age, he used to go to the Bangaru Kamakshi temple in Tanjavur and pour out his devotion.

Music became the medium for the expression of his devotion.

All of Syama Sastri's songs centre around his favourite Deity: *Kāmākshi,* the Divine Mother. He deemed himself as Her child. His musical compositions hence are marked by not only intense devotion, but also the spontaneity, simplicity and sincerity of a child addressing its mother.

Nadopasana or practice of music with devotion is an accepted means of God realisation and Syama Sastri, like the other two members of the trinity Tyagaraja and Muttuswami Dikshitar, proved through his life and work how simple and effective this could be.

TYAGARAJA

TYAGARAJA (1767-1847 A.D.)

Tyagaraja, the saint composer, was born in Tiruvaiyar in Tamil Nadu on 4th May 1767. He lived most of his life in Tiruvaiyar till his death on 6th January 1847.

Right from childhood he devoted himself to the worship of Lord Rama singing songs extolling his favourite deity.

He had a daughter, through whom he had a grandson, who died progeniless. Thus we do not have any descendants of saint Tyagaraja. His wife predeceased him.

Daily, Tyagaraja would walk the streets of his native town singing songs and seeking alms (known as *Unchavritti*).

Tyagaraja has composed about 800 songs, most of them in his mother tongue Telugu and a few in Sanskrit.

The only travel he undertook in his life was a short pilgrimage from Tirupati to Srirangam.

Tyagaraja shied away from material possessions and refused to sing in praise of the King. He was determined to remain poor and independent.

Tyagaraja lived his own philosophy that God realisation was best achieved through *Nādopāsanā* (music with devotion). His songs are surfeit with an intimate devotion for Rama, though they fully reveal his deep understanding of the tenets of the Vedas and Upanishads.

The music of his compositions overpowers the lyrical content, but there is no mistaking the spiritual effect of his songs on the listeners.

Purandharadasa was the grandfather of Carnatic music. Tyagaraja is one of its trinity, the other two being Muttuswami Dikshitar and Syama Sastri.

MUTTUSWAMI DIKSHITAR

MUTTUSWAMI DIKSHITAR (1775-1835 A.D.)

Like Tyagaraja and Syama Sastri, Muttuswami Dikshitar, one of the Trinity of Carnatic Music, was born in Tiruvarur in Tanjavur district of Tamil Nadu.

Inheriting music knowledge from his father, Muttuswami Dikshitar embellished it with his mastery of the Sanskrit language.

One special feature about the songs of Dikshitar is that they are all related to and centre around Deities in various temples in South India, to which he made pilgrimages throughout his life of sixty years.

Muttuswami Dikshitar composed his first song at the Subrahmanya temple at Tiruttani. He considered the Deity of this temple as his Guru and hence used the pen-name "*Guru Guha*" in all his musical compositions.

The major temples visited by Dikshitar and on whose deities he composed songs are: Tirupati, Kalahasti, Kancheepuram, Chidambaram, Madurai, Sri Rangam, Kumbakonam, Tirunelveli, Rameswaram, Tiruchendur, Sabarimalai apart from Tiruvarur, his own hometown.

Though Bhakti or devotion is the main ingredient in his songs, this is tempered by *Jnana* or knowledge.

Muttuswami Dikshitar was a Vedantin, in the tradition of Sankara, who believed in One Supreme Power and considered the deities worshipped as manifestations of that Supreme Power, who transcended name and form.

The songs of Dikshitar, composed in chaste Sanskrit and set to a variety of majestic tunes (both Carnatic and Hindustani), exude a feeling of serenity, dignity and bliss, characteristic of a truly evolved spiritual savant.

IRIYAMMAN TAMPI

IRIYAMMAN TAMPI (1782-1856 A.D.)

In devotional music, two names from Kerala stand out: Maharaja Swati Tirunal and Iriyamman Tampi.

While Swati Tirunal composed songs mainly in Sanskrit, Iriyamman Tampi's songs are mostly in Malayalam language. Though he frequently mixed Sanskrit and Malayalam in his compositions.

Iriyamman Tampi was born in Tiruvanantapuram, Kerala in 1782, in the royal family of Travancore.

His father was Kerala Varma Tampuran and his mother, Parvati Tankachi, daughter of the Maharaja's nephew.

His original name was Ravi Varma. This got corrupted into Iriyamman and the family title Tampi was added to it.

Iriyamman Tampi remained the Poet Laureate in the court of Swati Tirunal.

What is striking about the songs of Iriyamman Tampi—he composed 33 of them—is not only the easy flow of music, the simplicity of language or the delicacy of feeling, but the underlying deep rooted devotion to God which elevates them to a higher level.

Many of them are addressed to particular Deities in temples, like the Guruvayoor temple, Sri Padmanabhaswamy temple in Tiruvanantapuram and other temples in Kerala, the deities in which had a special fascination to the poet-devotee.

What has made Iriyamman Tampi immortal is his fascinating lullaby, "*Omanatingal kidavo*", in which he glorifies the manifestation of the Divine in every newborn child.

Iriyamman Tampi died in 1856, at the age of 75 years.

GOPALAKRISHNA BHARATI

GOPALAKRISHNA BHARATI (1810-1881 A.D.)

The songs of Gopalakrishna Bharati, the God-intoxicated Tamil composer, are remarkable for their intensity of devotion to Lord Siva, simplicity of diction and originality of rhythmic patterns.

He was born in 1810 A.D. in a village called *Narimanam* in Tanjavur district of Tamil Nadu. He lost his parents early in life and as an orphan was brought up and educated by relatives and friends.

Gopalakrishna Bharati was a great devotee of Siva and he was attracted by the stories about the Saivite saints: Nayanmars contained in the *Periya Puranam.* In particular, the life of Nandanar, the outcaste farm labourer who attained sainthood, appealed to him and made him create his magnum opus: *Nandanar Charitram,* the life of Nandanar, the songs from which have become popular all over Tamil Nadu and are part of the repertoire of every musician and dancer in South India.

The celestial dance of Nataraja, the Deity in the famous temple of Chidambaram, was the main inspiration for most of the songs of Gopalakrishna Bharati.

His fame spread even during his lifetime. There is a story that when he met the famous Tyagaraja, the latter asked him where he hailed from. When Gopalakrishna Bharati replied "I belong to Mayuram", Tyagaraja asked him if he knew about the famous musician Gopalakrishna Bharati. He had to say: "I am that humble self!"

Gopalakrishna Bharati lived a life of simplicity and frugality. He was a celibate all his life.

He had deep sympathy for the poor and downtrodden.

He died on the Sivaratri day in 1881.

He visited most of the Siva temples in the South, many of which inspired his moving mellifluous songs.

SWATI TIRUNAL

SWATI TIRUNAL (1813-1846 A.D.)

Maharaja Swati Tirunal lived only for a short period of 33 years but has bequeathed to us a veritable treasure of nearly 400 God-oriented songs, mostly in Sanskrit.

Swati Tirunal used to say: *All that I write, whether poetry or music centres round God. This is an act of faith with me. Music is not worth its name otherwise.*

Swati Tirunal was a contemporary of the Karnatic musical trinity: Tyagaraja, Muttuswami Dikshitar and Syama Sastri but did not meet any of them.

Ascending the throne at the age of sixteen, Swati Tirunal ruled over the state of Travancore for nearly 18 years till his death. He was an enlightened ruler and a patron of poets, artists and performers. Music was in his blood stream and many musicians flocked to his royal court. Interaction with the dance masters and dance troups from Tanjavur inspired Swati Tirunal to compose several forms of music for dance like *Tillanas, Varnas, Padas* and *Swarajatis.*

Swati Tirunal also imbibed the best from the many Hindustani musicians who flocked to his court and composed many songs in Hindustani ragas.

He was devoted to Lord *Padmanabha,* the deity in the Tiruvanantapuram temple, but he saw no distinction between Siva and Vishnu, whom he considered as two forms of the same Divinity. His famous song *Visvesvar darsan* exemplifies this philosophy of his.

Very few rulers could come anywhere near Swati Tirunal in his patronage of arts, his catholicity of religious outlook, his transcendence of narrow regional, religious and caste barriers. He was a truly evolved royal sage.

RAMALINGA SWAMIGAL

RAMALINGA SWAMIGAL (1823-1857 A.D.)

Ramalinga Swamigal, popularly known as *Vallalar*, was a poet and mystic who dreamt and sang of God as the eternal, effulgent Light.

He was born on 5th October 1823 A.D. in the village of Marudur, near Chidambaram, South India.

Though he lived only for 34 years, he had a powerful influence on 19th century India. He was a contemporary of Raja Ram Mohan Roy (1744-1832 A.D.), Ramakrishna Paramahamsa (1836-1886 A.D.) and Dayananda Saraswati (1824-1883 A.D.).

Ramalinga Swamigal composed 5818 devotional songs, compiled and published as "*Tiru Arut Pa*".

The *Tiru Arut Pa* is a monumental collection of devotional poetry, fully reflecting Ramalinga Swamigal's God intoxication and his total absorption in the Divine.

All the songs have spontaneity, emotional richness and mellifluous sweetness.

Ramalinga Swamigal stood for a universal religion, preaching compassion for all beings. He fought against all forms of discriminations based on birth, class, religion and caste.

He was for personal purity, sincerity and simple living.

His concern for the poor and downtrodden made him establish free poor feeding centres called *Satya Dharma Salas*.

In 1857, Ramalinga Swamigal attained Siddhi in Mettukuppam in a mysterious way. He locked himself in a room and when people opened the room there was nothing, no trace of his physical body. He had joined the Effulgent Light, *Arul perum Jyoti*, of which he sang all his life.

SRI RAMAKRISHNA PARAMAHAMSA

SRI RAMAKRISHNA PARAMAHAMSA (1836-1886 A.D.)

"God alone is the doer, and none else, that is knowledge. I am not the doer, I am a mere instrument in his hand. Therefore I say: "O Mother! Thou art the operator and I am the machine. Thou art the indweller and I am the House. Thou art the driver and I am the carriage. I move as Thou movest me. I do as Thou makest me do. I speak as Thou makest me speak. Not I, Not I, but Thou, but Thou" said the great God-intoxicated sage of Dakshineswar, Sri Ramakrishna.

As the brief introduction in the book *How God Came into My Life* puts it: "Starting as a poojari of the name of Gadadhar in a Kali temple, he developed into a prophet of universal religion. In an age of scepticism about the reality of the spirit, he made people see God with the certainty of science. A rare spiritual phenomenon of the nineteenth century he practised every *sādhanā* in a manner of one born to it and experienced all the *bhavas* of devotion. Embodying in himself every faith and creed, Sri Ramakrishna, by his practices and relisation, certified to the value and validity of all forms of approach to the Supreme."

Ramakrishna was born in the village of Kamarpukur in Hooghly District of Bengal on February 18, 1836 at about 6.30 a.m. to pious parents. Even from his childhood he was attracted by the lives of spiritual leaders. He had his first experience of spiritual ecstasy at the age of seven. He married at the age of 23 Saradamani Devi, but marriage did not, in any way, reduce his singleminded devotion to God.

Sri Ramakrishna felt that all religions were directing their steps to the same God. He himself had visions of Rama, Krishna, Siva, Kali, Allah and Jesus.

Sri Ramakrishna had a simple way of spiritually educating everyone through parables and anecdotes. He died of cancer on August 16, 1886 at the age of 51.

Sri Ramakrishna used to say: "The Self, the Supreme Self is the magnet, the individual self is the needle. The individual self experiences the state of Yoga when it is attracted by the Supreme Self to itself. But the magnet cannot attract the needle if the needle is covered with clay, it can draw the needle only when the clay is removed. The clay of "Woman" (lust) and "gold" must be removed. When you have thus freed yourself from impurity, you will be attracted by the magnet. Only then will you attain Yoga."

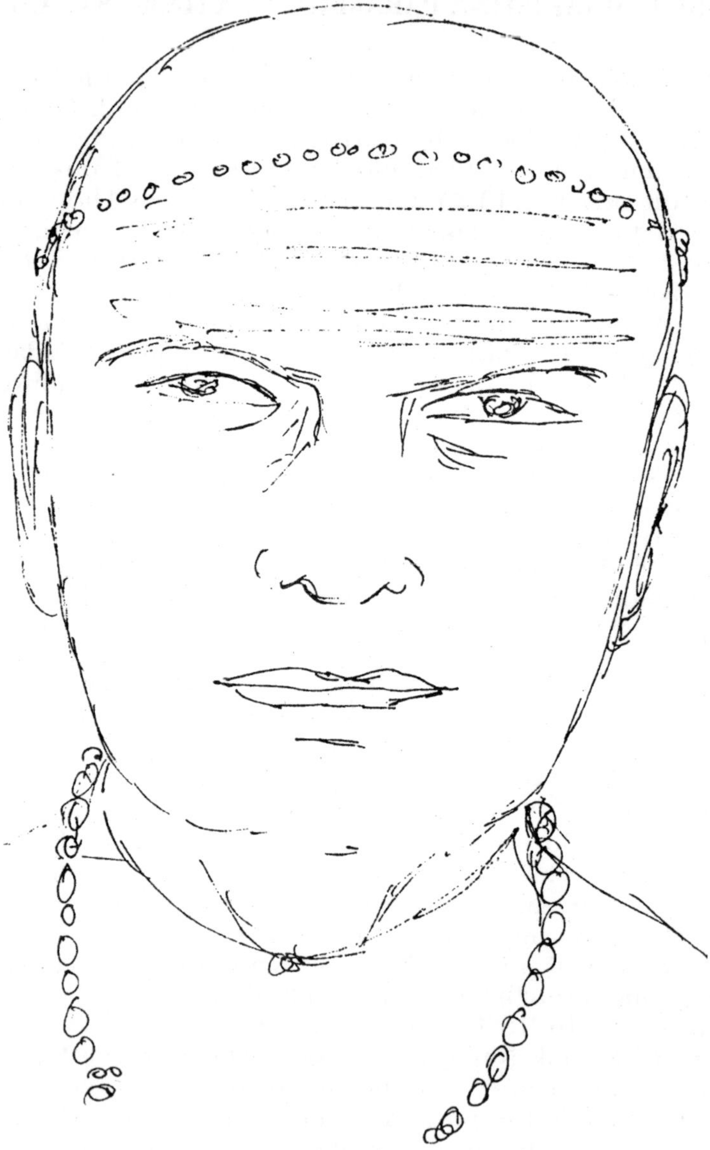

NEELAKANTHA SIVAN

NEELAKANTHA SIVAN (1839-1900 A.D.)

Neelakantha Sivan was a mystic, totally detached from worldly entanglements, though he was a married man with children and held the post of a village magistrate for 15 years.

Musical compositions flowed out of him, out of his spiritual inspiration and divine ecstasy. He has bequeathed over 1500 devotional songs to posterity.

Neelakantha Sivan was born in 1839 in Padmanabhapuram, capital of the erstwhile Travancore state in India.

At the age of 20, he joined Government service as a Village Magistrate, a job which he resigned after 15 years unable to compromise himself on a question of personal integrity. Thereafter he devoted himself wholly to composing devotional songs.

He visited most of the temples in South India and sang songs eulogizing the various Deities.

He died in 1900, at the age of 61. His last days were spent in Karamanai, Tiruvanantapuram.

Neelakantha Sivan's favourite Deity was Lord Siva, the Deity in the Padmanabhapuram temple, about 40 miles from Tiruvanantapuram, from whom he drew spiritual inspiration.

Most of his songs are dedications to Lord Siva.

The songs of Neelakantha Sivan in Tamil are similar to the Telugu compositions of Saint Tyagaraja. Both believed in *Nādopāsanā,* devotion through music.

Sivan used to organize *Bhajans* or collective singing of devotional songs at his residence to which people thronged to savour the ambience charged with spiritual fervour.

PATTANAM SUBRAMANIA IYER

PATTANAM SUBRAMANIA IYER (1845-1902 A.D.)

Pattanam Subramania Iyer, the great musical composer, was a disciple of the famous saint-composer Tyagaraja.

He was born in Tanjavur, Tamil Nadu in 1845 A.D. He studied music under his uncle, Melattur Ganapati Sastri and later under Venkatasubbaier.

He settled down in Tiruvaiyar (birthplace of Tyagaraja) and became a leading exponent of Carnatic music at the young age of 30 years.

The compositions of Pattanam Subramania Iyer are mainly in Telugu and Sanskrit. They follow the style of Tyagaraja. In fact, he earned the title *Chinna Tyagaraja* (Small Tyagaraja).

It is believed that Pattanam Subramania Iyer composed about 100 songs.

Most of his songs relate to his favourite Deity Lord Venkateswara of Tirupati (who is considered a manifestation of Sree Rama).

In all the songs there is an intimate appeal to the Lord to forgive and show mercy.

In particular, the song *Raghuvamsasuta* in the raga *Kathanakutoohalam* is a masterpiece and most popular among Carnatic singers today.

Pattanam Subramania Iyer died in Tiruvaiyar on July 31, 1902, at the age of 58 years.

BHIMA BHOI

BHIMA BHOI (1849-1894 A.D.)

Bhima Bhoi, the blind, tribal mystic of Orissa, is noted for his devotional songs in honour of God, the Unmanifest (*Nirākāra* or *Nirguna Brahman*).

The philosophy of Bhima Bhoi, termed "*Mahima Dharma*", extols God as the Unseen Power which pervades everything in the universe.

Bhima Bhoi was born in 1849 in a poor tribal family in the Diha village near Radhakol, Orissa. He was born blind.

Bhima Bhoi did not have any education.

Despite his physical handicap of blindness, Bhima Bhoi became a great poet of devotional songs (locally called *Bhajans*). These were sung by him and written down by his disciples, who popularised them among the people.

The songs have been compiled into a large number of books, chief among them being the *Bṛhat Bhajanamala* and *Stuti Chintamani.*

The followers of *Mahima Dharma* established by Bhima Bhoi could either be celibates or householders. Bhima Bhoi himself was a householder, having married a Brahmin girl named Annapurna, who bore him two children: a son named Kapileswar and a daughter named Labanybati. Bhima Bhoi died in 1894 at the age of 45.

Adoration of God as an invisible presence is unique in the Bhakti movement in India, where the other mystics poured out their love for specific manifestations of Divinity.

Bhima Bhoi's songs reveal a passionate yearning for God, the Invisible, Elusive One.

NARAYANA GURU

NARAYANA GURU (1856-1928 A.D.)

Narayana Guru, the poet-sage and mystic of Kerala, belongs to the band of spiritual teachers like Tirumoolar, Tiruvalluvar, Sri Ramakrishna Paramahamsa and Ramana Maharishi.

He was born on August 20, 1856 A.D. at Chenpazhanti, north of Tiruvanantapuram (the present capital of Kerala State) in an *Ezhava* family.

He studied Sanskrit under the famous Sanskrit scholar Kammanpally Raman Pillai.

Even from an early age, Nanoo (as he was affectionately called) was introspective and contemplative and preferred solitude and deep thought.

He left home and wandered from place to place in search of spiritual guides and holy places. He spent some time in a cave in a mountain called *Marutwamalai* in Tamil Nadu, where he is believed to have attained enlightenment.

Coming down from the seclusion of the mountain cave, Narayana Guru mixed with people of all castes and religions and proclaimed his famous dictum: "*One caste, one religion, one God for man*".

Like the Advaitic philosopher, Sankaracharya, Narayana Guru believed in the omnipresence and immanence of God.

In one of his songs, he asks God: "*Aren't you illusion, the creator of illusion, the one who sports with illusion and the one who removes illusion?*"

Again, like Sankaracharya, Narayana Guru has composed beautiful devotional songs to various manifestations of Divinity like Siva, Subrahmanya, Divine Mother, etc.

He attained samadhi on September 20, 1928 at Sivagiri.

RABINDRANATH TAGORE

RABINDRANATH TAGORE (1861-1941 A.D.)

Rabindranath Tagore, the first Indian to get the Nobel Prize for Literature, though a multifaceted creative genius was basically a mystic-philosopher-poet, who saw the universe with all its colour and beauty as the joyful expression and manifestation of God.

His songs are imbued with this message and soaked in the culture, tradition and philosophy of India.

The most important songs of Rabindranath Tagore are his God-oriented outpourings contained in his famous *Gitanjali,* which won him the Nobel Prize.

The songs of Tagore in original Bengali, sung all over Bengal in sweet melodious tones, are termed *Rabindra Sangeet* and are part of the psyche of the people of Bengal.

The same intensity of God-intoxication seen in other mystic saints who lived centuries earlier and were devoted to personified manifestations of God is seen in the songs of Tagore, though he did not limit his devotion and adoration to a particular form of Deity.

For him, God was omnipresent as the Supreme Power. Nor was he otherworldly. "*Deliverance is not for me in renunciation. I feel the embrace of freedom in a thousand bonds of delight*" was his message.

It is this approach—and the beauty of the Bengali language—that invests his songs with such captivating charm.

SWAMI VIVEKANANDA

SWAMI VIVEKANANDA (1863-1902 A.D.)

Swami Vivekananda, the passionate social reformer, and the chosen disciple of Ramakrishna Paramahamsa was a religious mystic as well.

He was born as Narendra Nath in Calcutta on 12 January, 1863 A.D. From a very early age, he had a leaning towards spirituality.

In 1881 he met Ramakrishna and at the very first meeting, the two took a liking to each other and they became Master and disciple. When the Master died in 1886, the mantle passed on to the disciple.

Vivekananda travelled widely, preaching Vedanta and the universality of religion.

He declared: "We have to learn that all religions, under whatever name they may be called, either Hindu, Buddhist, Mohammedan or Christian, have the same God, and he who derides any one of these derides his own God."

In 1893, Vivekananda addressed the Parliament of Religions in the United States and won wide acclaim.

His words appealed to all: "Through high philosophy or low, through the most exalted mythology or the grossest, through the most refined ritualism or arrant fetishism, every sect, every soul, every nation, every religion, consciously or unconsciously, is struggling upward, towards God, every vision of truth that man has is a vision of Him and of none else."

In 1892, he founded the Ramakrishna Mission which is spreading his message all across the world.

He died in 1902.

The songs of Vivekananda indicate his adoration of God, in the familiar manifestations of Divine Mother and Father.

MYSORE VASUDEVACHAR

MYSORE VASUDEVACHAR (1865-1961 A.D.)

Mysore Vasudevachar was a musical composer, who had realized Divinity as bliss and shared that bliss with others through his wonderful musical compositions.

Though he was a Kannadiga by birth, most of his compositions are in Sanskrit and a few in Telugu.

He was born on May 28, 1865 in Mysore.

He lost his father at the age of three and was brought up by his maternal grandfather. He learnt Sanskrit and music from a very early age.

At the age of 19, he went to Tiruvayyaru and became a disciple of the famous Pattanam Subramania Iyer and imbibed the musical tradition of his teacher.

Though he was a great singer and won wide acclaim as such, it is as a composer of great devotional songs that Mysore Vasudevachar will be remembered.

He has bequeathed about 200 songs in 100 different *ragas* (melodies) all of which are an invariable part of the repertoire of Carnatic musicians.

Like Neelakantha Sivan, Mysore Vasudevachar also used to organize *Bhajans* at his residence which were veritable musical feasts.

A few personal tragedies (he lost his wife at the age of 40 and his only daughter fell into a well and died) put an end to the residential *bhajans.*

But the Maestro continued to compose soulful songs and encouraged his disciples to hold *bhajans* at their homes, which he attended.

He died on May 17, 1961, by which time several titles and honours had come to him. Rabindranath Tagore called him: *"Sangeeta Kala Kovida".*

AUROBINDO GHOSH

SRI AUROBINDO GHOSH (1872-1950 A.D.)

Sri Aurobindo, the mystic philosopher saint of India, had three passions: love of God, love of man and love for India.

His outstanding contribution is his thesis *that human life can be made Life Divine even in the material world.*

Life has emerged from matter, and mind from life. The progress of evolution is a gradual emergence of consciousness. This cannot stop at the existing level of mental consciousness in man, but has to emerge into a Supermind, manifesting God's glory. Aurobindo distilled the wisdom of the ancient Indian scriptures like the *Vedas, Upanishads* and the *Bhagavat Gita* and gave his message for the spiritual regeneration of the world from his Ashram in Pondicherry.

Sri Aurobindo's most famous works are: *The Life Divine* (his materpiece), *Savitri, The Ideal of Human Unity,* and *Integral Yoga.*

The essence of his teachings is: *God must be realised not beyond the universe but in the universe, not only in the soul but in the human body, not only as Spirit but as Matter. Life is the field for the progressive manifestation of God. Man, through Divine Grace, must evolve into Superman.*

Sri Aurobindo was born on August 15, 1872 in Calcutta. After schooling in Darjeeling in 1879 he went with his family to England. After finishing his studies, he returned to India in 1893 and joined the Baroda State Service. For the next 17 years, in Baroda and later in Calcutta as Principal, National College, he worked for Indian Independence. In 1908 he left politics and in 1910 went to Pondicherry where he lived till his death on December 5, 1950.

Aurobindo, who had mastered Yoga, set up an Ashram in Pondicherry which has become an international centre of spiritual culture and research.

HARIKESANALLUR MUTHIAH BHAGAVATAR

HARIKESANALLUR MUTHIAH BHAGAVATAR (1877-1945 A.D.)

Spirituality is inherent in Indian music and when the melodies or *Rāgas* are linked to words eulogizing some manifestation of God, a devotional song results, elevating the listener to heights of spiritual bliss.

Harikesanallur Muthiah Bhagavatar's proficiency in music, combined with his background as a *Harikatha* performer (one who narrates religious stories musically), enabled him to bequeathe some outstanding musical compositions which provide the listener not only aesthetic satisfaction but spiritual bliss as well.

Muthiah Bhagavatar was born on November 15, 1877 at a village near Srivilliputhur. When he was six, his father died and he came under the care of his maternal uncle at Harikesanallur.

In 1886, he went to Tiruvaiyar to study Vedas, but soon switched to study of Carnatic music.

After completing his studies he returned in 1893 to Harikesanallur and started performing music concerts.

In 1897, he gave a recital before the Maharaja of Travancore and got royal patronage.

From 1904, he began performing *Harikathas* and composing devotional songs called *Kirtanas.*

In 1927, the Mysore Maharaja appointed him as a chief musician.

In 1936, he went to Travancore. In 1943, he returned to Mysore and died there on June 30, 1945.

Muthiah Bhagavatar was one of the most outstanding composers of Carnatic music, after the Trinity of Tyagaraja, Muttuswami Dikshitar and Syama Sastri.

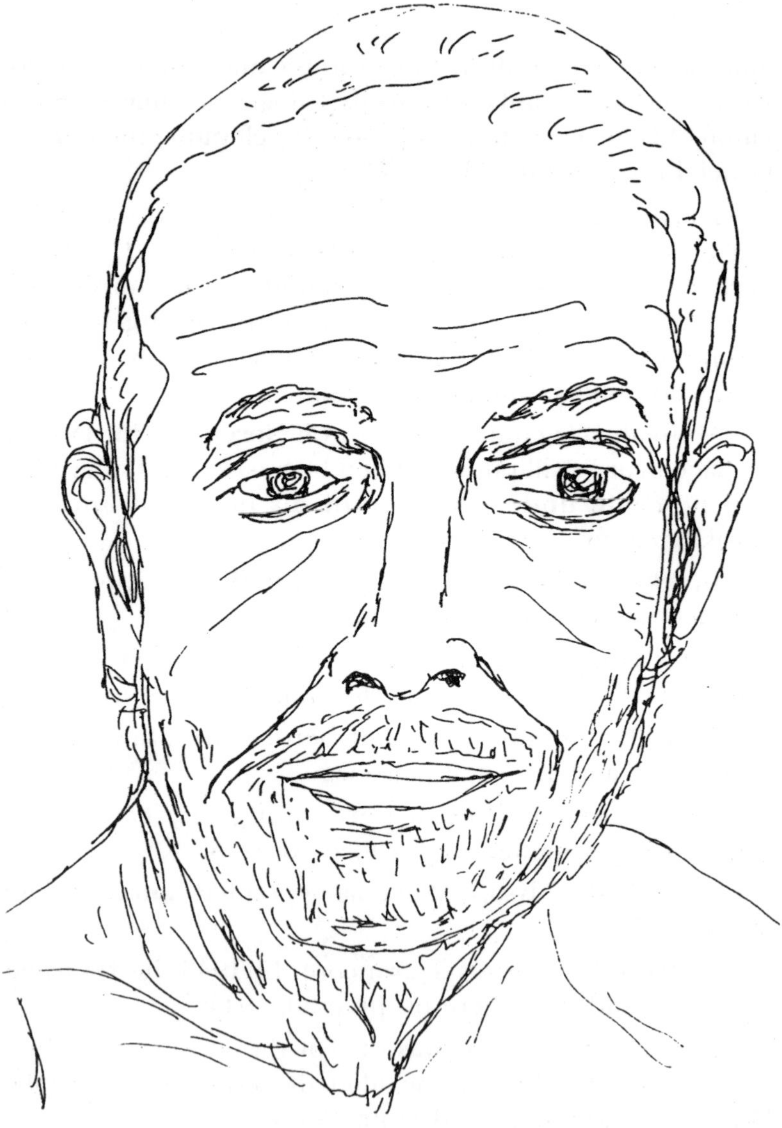

RAMANA MAHARISHI

RAMANA MAHARISHI (1879-1950 A.D.)

Sri Ramana Maharishi, the Sage of Arunachala, a powerful spiritual dynamo preaching the secrets of Vedantic wisdom, was born on December 30, 1879, seven years before the samadhi of Sri Ramakrishna.

He ran away from home at the age of 17, in search of true reality and reached Tiruvannamalai or Arunachala.

In the note which he left behind while leaving home, he wrote: "I leave in search of my father. According to his command, on a virtuous enterprise indeed, I have this day embarked. Therefore, for this action none need grieve nor trace this one. No money need be spent for my search."

Later, experiencing advaitic *anubhava* and living in *sahaja* samadhi as a *Jivanmukta,* he proclaimed: "The material body dies, but the spirit transcending it cannot be touched by death. I am therefore the deathless spirit."

He gave up his earthly body in 1950 at the age of 71.

"The one Self, the Supreme Self pervades everything. There exists no second permanent being" proclaims Advaita philosophy which was lived, preached and practised by Sri Ramana Maharishi.

Both Ramakrishna and Ramana Maharishi were pure needles, untainted by lust and gold, from their very childhood. That is why, they were so effortlessly drawn to the Supreme Self, the magnet.

SUBRAMANIA BHARATI

SUBRAMANIA BHARATI (1882-1921 A.D.)

Subramania Bharati, the doyen of Tamil poets, was a philosopher, besides being an ardent patriot of the pre-Independence era in India. Though he lived only a short life of 39 years, his poetic output was prodigious.

Subramania Bharati was a deeply religious person, though he did not believe in orthodoxy and rigidities of caste distinctions.

He believed in the brotherhood of mankind and considered God as the Supreme Power manifesting as and guiding the universe. Though he was an *advaitin* at heart, he also believed in the various manifestations of Divinity as Krishna, Muruga, Ganesa, Devi or Shakti etc.

His devotional songs are a veritable granary of devotion and spirituality.

Bharati's approach to God has similarities with that of Rabindranath Tagore. Like the latter, he also saw the universe with all its colour and beauty as the joyful expression and manifestation of God.

But unlike Tagore, Bharati, in the tradition of the earlier mystic saints, was also devoted to personal manifestations of God.

PAPANASAM SIVAN

PAPANASAM SIVAN (1890-1973 A.D.)

Papanasam Sivan, the Tamil music composer, has been termed "Tamil Tyagaraja".

His musical compositions, mainly in Tamil and numbering over 2000, are surcharged with devotion to God in His various manifestations.

He was born in Polagam village in Tanjavur district.

His original name was Ramaiah, and in many of his songs, he has inserted his pen-name as "Ramadasa". But because he lived for some time in Papanasam and was attired like a Saivite devotee, wearing *rudraksha* and holy ashes, he came to be known as "*Papanasam Sivan*".

Sivan was fond of conducting Bhajans and visited the various temples of Tamil Nadu, singing soul-stirring songs.

From 1930, he started living in Mylapore, Madras. He was specially attached to the Lord in the Kapali temple and many of his most heartrending devotional songs centre around the Deities in this temple: *Lord Kapali* and *Mother Karpagam.*

Sivan lived upto the age of 83 years and till his death on 1st October, 1973 kept himself busy composing and singing the glories of his beloved Deities. He freely mixed Sanskrit with Tamil in his songs, which are a perfect combination of *Bhakti, Rāga, Sangeeta* and *Sāhitya.*

SRI CHANDRASEKHARA SARASWATI

SRI CHANDRASEKHARA SARASWATI—PARAMACHARYA OF KANCHI (1894-1994 A.D.)

The Paramacharya of Kanchi, who became a *Sannyasin* at the tender age of 13 and lived almost 100 years, was an embodiment of simplicity, self-effacement and intense spirituality.

For 87 years he lived as the spiritual heir of Adi Sankara, kindling spiritual awakening in millions by his sheer presence. He broke his silence as a recluse—calling it a step down—to deliver spiritual discourses to explain his cardinal message that righteousness—the source of universal peace and prosperity—should be made to prevail and not lose out to forces of darkness.

Paramacharya was born on May 6, 1894 and was a student at a Christian Mission School in Tindivanam, when the call to be a *Sannyāsi* came in 1907.

Paramacharya's spiritual aura attracted people all over the world, irrespective of religion or country.

Many epithets have been used to refer to his strong spiritual attraction. These include: "*Moral Monarch, Divine Integrator* and *Manifestation of God that walks*" (the Tamil words being *Nadamaadum daivam*).

Paramacharya's discourses have been compiled into 7 bulky volumes and titled "*The Voice of God*".

The Dalai Lama referred to him as "my Elder brother in religion".

The Paramacharya once said: "Life has taught me only this: *God has created some souls to live for others only.*"

His own life was an example of the lesson Life taught him.

Paramacharya attained Samadhi on January 1, 1994.

JIDDU KRISHNAMURTHY

JIDDU KRISHNAMURTHY (1895-1986 A.D.)

Jiddu Krishnamurthy, the philosopher from India, was a revolutionary thinker. He negated all that had been taken for granted: the Guru, the master, the pupil, the book, the ideal.

He held that total responsibility lies with the individual. He talked of a *New Mind.*

His view was that in the world of today most people are second-hand human beings, followers of some leader or ideology. If the problems facing the world like the various conflicts between human beings and assault of Nature by technology and industry—have to be resolved, there has to be a change in the individual consciousness.

Krishnamurthy's philosophy envisages the emptying of the individual consciousness of all its beliefs, ideas, ideologies, memories and thoughts which would result in an emptiness—a stilled mind—a great silence—a space charged with powerful energy. This mutation of the individual's consciousness will transform the society as a whole. *New minds will create new Men and new men will create a new society.*

Jiddu Krishnamurthy was born in Madras (now called Chennai), India in 1895. He was educated in England by Dr. Annie Besant, who in 1925 proclaimed him as the *Messiah.* Krishnamurthy rejected the title and travelled the world, teaching and advocating a way of life and thought, unconditioned by the narrowness of nationality, race and religion, till his death in 1986 at age 91.

He wrote several books, expounding his philosophy. He preached compassion. He said: "To go far you have to travel light and shed your pettiness and your anger and your resentment." His was a life-enhancing philosophy, which *upheld the sacred in the universe, moral freedom and exemption from all kinds of prejudice.*

SUDDHANANDA BHARATI

SUDDHANANDA BHARATI (1897-1937 A.D.)

Suddhananda Bharati was a multifaceted personality: a patriot, poet, Yogi and a mystic God-intoxicated devotee.

He was born on 11th May 1897 at Sivaganga in Ramnad district of Tamil Nadu. From an early age he was moved by the tales of sages and saints and preferred a spiritual life to material riches.

Deeply influenced by the singing of devotees in the Meenakshi Temple in Madurai, he took a vow to compose devotional songs himself—a vow which he more than fulfilled in later life.

The name *Suddhananda* (lit. the blissful, pure soul) was given to him by his Guru, when he was hardly nine years old.

A meeting with Mahatma Gandhi in 1914 led to his involvement in politics for some time, but a vision of *Bhārata Śakti* which he had at Tuticorin, turned him from politics to the spiritual world.

He spent 23 years at Sri Aurobindo Ashram in Pondicherry and perfected his mastery of Yoga. His philosophy of spiritual yoga was derived from Sri Aurobindo. This has been fully expounded in his magnum opus *Bhārata Śakti,* rich in allegory and symbolism.

The songs of Suddhananda Bharati reveal his devotion to God, expressed in mellifluous Tamil poetry, reminiscent of the other shorter-lived poet of the same genre, Subramania Bharati.

God, to Suddhananda Bharati, was: "*The apple of his eye, Life of his life, who dances in the hearts of his devotees.*"

The pure nectar of devotion, rich imagery and the exquisite quality of the Tamil language make his songs so charming and popular.

INDEX